SECRETS OF THE STONES

SECRETS OF

THE STONES

Decoding Ireland's lost past

ROB VANCE

ashfield
PRESS

Published in 2009 by
ASHFIELD PRESS • DUBLIN • IRELAND

ISBN: 978-1-901658-73-6

CERTIFIED
CARBON
NEUTRAL®
Publication
CarbonNeutral.com
CO₂ emissions reduced to
net zero in accordance with
The CarbonNeutral Protocol

This book is typeset by Ashfield Press
in 11.5 on 14 point Quadraat and Biggs

Designed by SUSAN WAINE
Printed in Ireland by GPS COLOUR GRAPHICS LIMITED, BELFAST

CONTENTS

PREFACE
7

FOREWORD BY PETER HARBISON
8

CHAPTER 1
KNOWTH TO MELLIFONT
11

CHAPTER 2
EARLY BEGINNINGS
24

CHAPTER 3
MEGALITHIC TOMBS
40

CHAPTER 4
THE TOMBS OF THE BOYNE VALLEY
53

CHAPTER 5
FROM THE EARTH TO THE SKY
72

CHAPTER 6
THE HILL OF TARA
89

CHAPTER 7
MEDIEVAL IRELAND
119

CHAPTER 8
CLONMACNOISE
145

RECOMMENDED READING
169

INDEX
173

TELEVISION PROGRAMME CREDIT LIST
180

PREFACE

THIS BOOK AND SERIES began as a result of Colm Crowley and I working together on a number of history and archaeology television series. We often wished we could bring long-vanished buildings back to life, having filmed ruined sites with good stories; but with no structures visible, the television audience sometimes had to imagine what had once been there. In many cases, there was only a grassy surface.

I had written about and photographed Irish antiquities for a number of books and when Colm suggested using computer-generated imagery [CGI] to rebuild important sites, we had a TV series location-list within a day. Peter Harbison gave expert opinion, and we put together a presentation document and five-minute pilot-script, which helped raise the finance.

The television series became *Secrets of the Stones* and this accompanying book sketches the background and beliefs of those who designed and built the ancient and medieval buildings which feature in the programmes. Arguably, these structures are part of who we are, and give a grounding to Irish identity. The ones that still lie buried could one day be rebuilt.

For inclusiveness, I have selected artefacts from different parts of the country, which fit the time-scale of the featured sites. I have also filled the several millennia between Knowth and Mellifont with high-definition frames taken from the series, old Irish astronomical manuscripts and many of my photographs, to part-explain at least, the complex and enigmatic society shown in the two episodes.

To write a book and take the associated photographs in a short time needed help and that was given in generous amounts. As well as many of those mentioned in Colm's introduction on front flap, I also add David and Catherine Gibson-Brabazon, who allowed us to film the five-minute pilot at Mount Dalton and who gave this writer sustenance during the writing of the book. Kevin McGilligan accompanied me on many of the photographic trips and was, as always, a sturdy assistant and entertaining companion.

Claudia Kohler of the Kerry County Museum lent excellent photographs, and Petra Schnabel of the Royal Irish Academy was patient in gathering the right manuscripts and illustrations. Peter Harbison kindly read the text and his suggestions were perceptive and illuminating.

My thanks also to John Davey of Ashfield Press for turning the book around in double-quick time and to Susan Waine for a superb design.

Opposite page:
A detail of a decorative pig playing bagpipes in the 16th century Dinshencheas, or Lore of Placenames

Library of the Royal Irish Academy

◄

7

FOREWORD

ARCHAEOLOGY IS A HUMAN SCIENCE that never stands still. All over the world, a variety of disciplines combine daily to shed new light on our ancestors and where we came from. Ireland's past has been the beneficiary of some of these new researches, and Colm Crowley of RTE Cork cleverly pressed them into service for television to provide us with a new vision of the often astounding achievements of the country's prehistoric and medieval people.

This encompasses fascinating recent findings on the building of Sligo's Megalithic tombs ahead of the Pharaohs, the erection of what sounds like a monumental wooden version of Stonehenge, now hidden beneath the soil of Tara's royal hill, the discovery of Ireland's first known church in a Kerry valley and documenting the similarities between individual stone High Crosses on the venerable monastic sites of Clonmacnoise and Durrow.

Under the direction of Lisa Harney and Julian Thomas, a team of leading

Centaurs parade along the base of the Market Cross at Kells., Co. Meath

scholars and scientists were assembled to present two programmes on these surprising new developments in the study of Ireland long ago, and RTE Cork encouraged the production of a book which would create a more permanent record. John Davey of Ashfield Press took up the challenge and commissioned Rob Vance, himself a presenter of classic TV programmes unearthing Ireland's often quirky past, to create a beautifully illustrated volume presenting some of the programme's prime features and placing them in the framework of their historic and pre-historic background. Rob tells it with his own inimitable brand of personal enthusiasm for the subject, allowing himself imaginative insights which he intersperses between quotes from the experts who participated in the programmes. After this, our vision of Ireland's past will never be the same again!

PETER HARBISON, 2009

An Iron-Age stone in the
Church of Ireland
Cathedral at Armagh

KNOWTH
TO MELLIFONT

1

THIS BOOK and television series primarily looks at sites which could be said to be iconic, a word grossly overused, yet in its true sense a representation of something holy imbued with meaning and perhaps magic. By this definition, many of our featured sites have that quality. Some, like the Hill of Tara, have had it since before the written word and its power remains strong, resonating through time, bringing thousands to its rampart, defending against the mohair-suited *Firbolg* of today.

The stones of the distant past are more than objects, not just rocks or old buildings. Structures built thousands of years ago speak to our ancient imagination, as if some vestigial meaning remains within their primal belly shape and uterine interiors. Yet, even with our technology, they defy us to find meaning in their symbols and carvings. For many today, a cathedral is no different, a complex structure from a distant time, relating to birth, death and the rituals involved. It is also something from the ancient past.

The first structures the book and series explore come from the Stone Age, a time seemingly dominated by a religious attachment to the earth itself, whose nature, or innate spirit, was perceived as a 'Great Mother' of the tribe. There is much evidence to suggest that such a deity was worshipped in one form or another across much of the Neolithic world and

A carved stone figure from Armagh, traditionally Labhraidh Loingseach, ancestor god of the Leinster tribal groups ➤

her cult may have been widely spread throughout many communities. At its heart was a concept of the earth as maternal and nurturing, but also capricious and devouring.

We know very little about what the tomb-builders thought, because at some-time in the distant past, their mysterious and complex society suffered collapse and they closed the tombs and disappeared from the record. Something more powerful than the gods in whom they believed arrived in the sky and turned their world upside down. That ancient yet sophisticated society with its division of labour and developing astro-science, vanished as a dominant group, leaving burnt bones, necklaces and a mace-head. They did not continue in power into the Bronze Age. Something changed their belief-system for ever and reassembling the remaining fragments of their past is like putting together a mosaic with many pieces missing. But through examining physical remains and deciphering the pieces of stone, we may answer some of the questions raised about Irish pre-history. Facts now suggest that sudden and severe climate change may have been the catalyst for immense social upheaval in Ireland but also across Europe. Part of the answer is trapped in ice-cores and in preserved trees from under the midland bogs. Atmospheric dust in ice-core bubbles, frozen 4,000 years ago, tell what happened. Tree-ring data confirm a severe climate downturn, with disastrous results.

An Irish warrior with sword and shield from the south cross at Castledermot, Co. Kildare

The people of the Stone Age may have seen the movements of the sun and moon and the recurring seasons as no more than the benevolent whim of a capricious god or goddess. Returning yearly warmth and the growth of crops were obviously linked but might have seemed dependent on 'keeping in' with your deity. This might have involved human and animal sacrifice, but the ancient past hides its secrets well. Some we shall never recover. Other questions arise...The Boyne Valley tombs were larger and bigger than anything required to house merely bones, so what happened inside the tombs? Was it ritual death, or royal birth surrounded by tribal symbols? Certain experts believe they were not tombs in the general sense of the word, but rather were shrines to ancestors and that those buried were more likely sacrificial victims than descendants of the surrounding farming community. Perhaps early society was cumulatively more violent than today. The lives of these people, as evidenced by the recovered, carbon-dated bones, were short and often brutal. Yet they had mathematics, organisation and a stylised art that came from Brittany and the Atlantic coast of Europe.

The landscape of pre-historic Ireland was very different to today's. It would be physically unrecognisable to us, more like northern Canada with vast forests intercut with rivers, mountain and bog, a wilderness alive with deer, wild boar, bears, eagles, wolves and scattered human settlements, initially in coastal areas. There were no roads and very few people. The communities did not grow to any huge population and from the time of the dolmens to the 12th century when the Normans arrived, the entire population was never more than 500,000.

But if today we have many ways in which to make sense of our lives be that religion, yoga or diet, the beliefs and mysteries of pre-historic people may have been similar in some ways at least. They had an integrated political-eco-system that ran smoothly, but in parts of the world, if the system failed, they deposed the king and got a better one. Perhaps Ireland was similar. The religion of these people was probably part entertainment, part horror story and part pep talk. Fear and spectacle work together in societies where there is danger from within, or a perceived threat from a foreign source. Having strong and powerful gods made people feel good about themselves and capable of resisting invaders or other threats. Having a god who returned every year to warm the soil and bring life was a good god to have on your side. But everything changes when what you believe in collapses, or when the climate goes awry, as it did several times in the distant past.

Another severe climatic event in the 6th century may have assisted the conversion of Ireland to Christianity because again the change of climate could have heralded the arrival of a new god and the defeat of the older ones. However, the success of that social and belief system brought fundamental change to Ireland. It ushered in fresh ideas, new modes of thought, and created an outlet for the Gaelic intellectual elite, many of whom became the monks and abbots of the new faith. Metalworking was revived, decorated manuscripts were created, and Irish monks travelled across Europe, earning an enviable reputation in their newly acquired Latin, Greek and Philosophy. Christianity found a fertile soil in Ireland.

Following page: A page of delicate calligraphy from the 14th century Book of Ballymote which moved from its traditional keepers, the MacDonagh family to Aodh O'Donell, prince of Tyrconnell, for the sum of 40 milch cows. *Library of the Royal Irish Academy Royal*

THE WRITTEN WORD

The long Gaelic oral tradition, whereby law, medicine, genealogy and poetry were memorised over decades, became the new 'written' word, first in Latin and then in Irish, a language that stretched back to Indo-European antiquity. But as writing in Irish began, in order perhaps to squeeze more words onto a vellum (calfskin) page, the monks adapted the standard *scriptura franca*, the uncial 'typeface' of the Roman Empire, and created a smaller script called half-uncial, with its own idiosyncratic usage and style. They used it for important manuscripts and adopted an even smaller, more squat letter-form for everyday use. And so Irish, the oldest vernacular language in Western Europe, became a written language, its tales and legends whispering of Sanskrit, Hindu king-rituals and a culture untouched by Rome and the Caesars. But Irish monks, chosen perhaps from the ranks of long-established Irish intellectual families, were no mere clerics doing others' bidding. As they became proficient in Latin, they decided to create something new and revolutionary, a Latin grammar book for beginners, a sort of 7th-century *Latin for Dummies*, and used it to teach people who had never seen the language before. It was the first basic grammar book of that language anywhere.

Within a century or so of coming into contact with Latin, the Irish had become experts in that language, writing in a style that outshone many in Europe who had grown up with Latin. They also developed clever ideas about putting words on a page with clarity and style. They invented the *page layout*, as we understand it today, using capital letters to start sentences, full-stop punctuation, the superscript 'dash' and word separation. These changes were hugely innovative and are still used today.

A medieval font from the site of the monastery of Clonard in County Meath, important as a seat of church power and pilgrimage with metal work-shops and houses…yet its precise location remains unknown

▼

For several hundred years, early Christian Ireland was the medieval equivalent of Silicon Valley, a powerhouse of new ideas, high-quality goods and occasional violence. Rivalry between monasteries could lead to attacks and assaults, yet these were usually resolved through the functioning and humane Brehon Law system, dating to the centuries before Christianity arrived in Ireland. Trade and commerce grew rapidly, as Christianity prospered, and helped create the monastic 'city' of Clonmacnoise where jewellers, metalworkers, scribes and monks built a wealthy society with the trappings of urban life before the plundering Scandinavians arrived. Ireland was an intellectual and commercial powerhouse during that time and the Irish pagan mind found in Christianity the medium and discipline for producing great art and expressed that creativity in sublime pieces of calligraphy, manuscript illumination and stone carving. Some of those involved were unsurpassed in what they did. They were the best in the known world.

The arrival of the Cistercian monks in 1147 brought Ireland into deeper contact with the forces that were shaping Europe. By the end of the 12th century, fundamental changes had ended Ireland's isolation from European politics.

The crozier stone from Boyle Abbey in Roscommon shows the independence of the monasteries and the power of the abbotts

EARLY BELIEFS

Irish pagan gods and goddesses lived in a parallel world with its own customs and politics, and many were patrons of metalworkers and skilled work in general. A god like 'Lugh', who gives his name to Lughnasa, the 1 August Celtic celebration, was popular across Europe, giving his name to Lyon in France, Leiden in Holland and Leibnitz in Silesia.

But Lugh may have been physically big in the sky, a prehistoric extra-terrestrial. Like Cu Chulainn, he may have arrived in Europe in the form of a comet, because many descriptions of these gods suggest their fiery shape and explosive nature.

A horned figure, perhaps the god Cernunnos decorates the side of the North cross at Clonmacnoise.

19

But if the sky is the source for new gods, then they require somewhere to be venerated and the Irish of the later Bronze Age created imposing timber and thatch structures, the equal of anything in pagan Europe. There is evidence to suggest that one huge building was 15 metres to the roof. The burnt foundations of this huge temple lie under the clay in County Armagh.

Yet we may have something more from the past than charred remains. There are many ways in which times long ago speak. Where the human voice is long vanished, other, older voices may be heard, speaking as it were through the stones. Our pre-literate ancestors had many ways of communicating, and the symbols and inscriptions left behind give us a clue about their beliefs. Their marks are enigmatic, more symbolic than linguistic in their representation, but evocative and inspiring nonetheless.

The idea of showing the human form does not generally appear in Irish art until the Christian period, but the rock carvings of the earlier passage tombs express a human understanding of the forces of nature and the cosmos. Astronomy was part of their lives, the observation of celestial movement a nightly theatre. Only when one is in a 'dark' part of this

Symbols of the sun and moon adorn a 17th century tomb-chest in St Multose's Church, Kinsale, Co Cork

increasingly bright and over-lit world does one appreciate the stunning panorama of the night sky, where galaxies and stars appear as they did to our ancestors. To witness a shooting star or something closer would have been awe-inspiring, if not terrifying. Celestial phenomena may have contributed to major social change at several times during Ireland's early history.

Many of the locations featured in this book reveal that our ancestors used stone and timber with creativity and great dexterity. Early societies on this island built huge tombs to honour their dead and later societies created timber structures to state their beliefs and reinforce their sense of belonging. The stone dwellings, the beehives of Skellig Michael are still dry after 1,400 years. Each era of tomb-building, temple construction and church-building, was executed with extraordinary skill and care. The people who built Newgrange or the hidden temple under the Hill of Tara were no Neanderthals throwing twigs on a fire. They had ingenuity, imagination and a sense of aesthetics. The later monks were no different.

LiDAR

N ew technology has dramatically reduced the time needed for an archaeological survey. A LiDAR (see page 102) 'photograph' of the Hill of Tara takes thousands of radar measurements in a short period of time that would involve several years of similar work on the ground. An electromagnetic beam finds the foundation trench for a huge, undisturbed and unknown circular temple under the hill. The blackened timber socketholes give a radio carbon date of 2,500 years ago. Complex royal sites that commanded vast areas of rich farmland can now be visually recreated.

New archaeological surveying techniques make it possible to study ancient sites without the need for excavation. We now can reveal, as never

A enigmatic human figure, perhaps medieval, lies embedded in a wall in County Westmeath

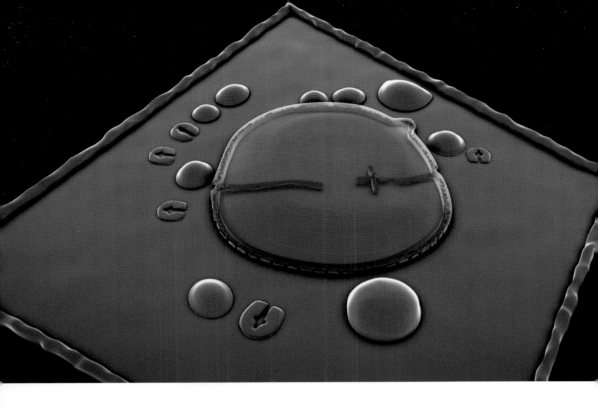

▲
· · · · · · · · · · · · · · · · · · · ·
This detailed
topographical
image of Knowth
is based on LiDar
data, obtained
through helicopter
laser scanning

before, the underlying secrets of Ireland's most enigmatic monuments. The footprint of another temple lies beneath the soil in County Kildare and its phases show a structure not unlike a sports stadium of today, semi-circular, with tiered seating and a special approach avenue for participants and spectators. The remains of huge feasts were found, with 18,000 pieces of animal bone buried in pits.

What lies beneath the surface of Ireland however, is coming to light more and more. Gaelic dynastic strongholds, high ramparts of earth over

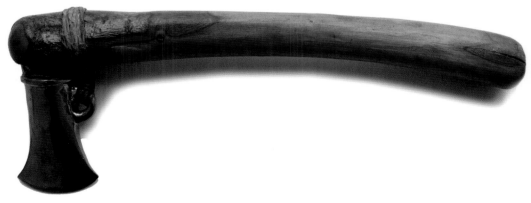

a thousand years old emerge from the road-digger's blade. The irony of road-building and general industrialisation is that 'progress' has unwittingly become a somewhat brutal discovery project. The positive side is that hundreds of archaeologists now scour the soil ahead of developments and add to our understanding of the times that preceded our own.

Bronze Age arrow and shaft from the Kerry County Museum

Opposite page: A replica Bronze Age handled axe from the Kerry County Museum

2

EARLY BEGINNINGS

Neolithic scrapers
for cleaning
animal skins from
County Kerry

· · · · · · · · · · · · · · · · · · · ·
▼

IRELAND IS FIRST AND FOREMOST one of a pair of islands in the Atlantic. It lies west of the continent of Europe and, over the millennia, art, trade, population and ideas from that vast land area has affected both islands and created their population. But thousands of years before any human foot stepped on this island, it was twice covered by glaciers, firstly 200,000 years ago and again 85,000 years after that. Some of the ice-caps may have been 300 metres thick, although we have been ice-free now for 10,000 years. During those periods,

woolly mammoth, brown bear, giant Irish deer, wolves and arctic foxes traversed the frozen landscape. As the glaciers began their final retreat, they smoothed the mountains and left a rich depth of glacial mud and clay which later became the best cattle-land in Europe. Southerly winds brought seeds and pollen from Iberia to Ireland and, as the climate changed towards a warm period, trees such as dwarf willow, juniper and birch began to cover the land. Around 8,000 years ago, oak and elm reached Ireland as the climate warmed further, to reach temperatures similar to today.

EARLY COMMUNITIES

From about 7,000 BC onwards, agriculture began to evolve from the growing of small pockets of cereal crops into cultivation, as new techniques arrived via Greece and the Balkans. No one is quite sure how the techniques of food production spread through the continent, but by 4,000 BC, wheat and barley were being grown along the Danube and the river valleys of central Europe. Those farming communities lived in rectangular houses, roughly 6.5 m by 6 m, built using timber posts hammered into wall trenches and filled with split logs. The house contained a hearth and a rubbish pit.

A pigs jaw from a Neolithic site in County Kerry

Ireland's oldest human remains are Europeans who hunted and trapped their way through what is now Scotland and sailed the narrow channel that separated the two islands around 8,000 years ago. Their middens (domestic refuse) along the vanished shores of lakes and disappeared shore-lines, show that their diet was based on shellfish and sea-fish, with occasional wild pig or duck.

They lived primarily around the coast of what is now Antrim and along the shore of several huge lakes in the midlands. Lough Derravaragh in County Westmeath is the remnant of one of these giant lakes. Another is Ardee Bog in modern County Louth, which covered over 25 square kilometres until its exploitation by state bodies. Several finds of Irish giant deer skeletons have been made where the lake formerly stood. The people then were hunter-gatherers, fishing salmon with bone harpoons and also trapping birds such as mallard, teal and widgeon with woven nets. They stored hazelnuts, a rich source of winter protein, and caught wild pig, which they roasted. Their homes were small huts, similar in shape to a half-coconut, usually with a hearth near the centre and made by ramming saplings in the ground and bending them over to form a round shape. These beehives were covered in animal skins or turves.

Initially, the first bands of hunters camped around the shore of those great midland lakes and constructed *Fulacht Fiadh*, a device for boiling venison or pork. The cooking was done by digging a shallow trench, lining it with timber to make a trough, heating stones and dropping them into the water until it boiled. This was tested by archaeologists in the 1940s and found to be an efficient and succulent way of cooking a piece of meat wrapped in straw.

For several thousand years these tiny communities were the only people on an island alive with game of every kind: deer, boar, salmon, wild pig and some competing predators, such as eagles and wolves. A community lived where Howth is today when the peninsula was an island and a shell midden, a Neolithic rubbish heap, revealed discarded shells from limpets, mussels, cockles, scallops and oysters. Other middens revealed the discarded bones of brown bear, grey seal, goat, pig and a small terrier type dog, probably domesticated. The surrounding countryside had elm and oak forest

Shells from the typical diet of the Stone Age

26

A Romanesque mask, like some ancient god, glowers from the chancel arch of St Mary's Cathedral, Tuam

Following page:
A Computer
Generated Image
of a monument at
Carrowmore,
possibly the largest
megalithic
cemetary in Europe
at one time

stretching to the lakes of the midlands, while pine was the main timber to the north. In pre-history, Ireland had many giant forests and the area covered by today's counties of Sligo and Roscommon had woods spread over thousands of square kilometres, a huge forest that stretched along the western bank of the Shannon as far as Athlone.

By 3000 BC, it was 2.5 degrees Celsius warmer than today and, perhaps owing to population increase or other social pressures, new population groups sought the island at the edge of the world. They brought the first domestic animals, tying down cattle with ropes of human hair in hide boats like the currachs of Ireland's west coast. It took several journeys to reach Ireland, perhaps from Brittany to Cornwall, then to south Wales before they explored the Irish coast for a safe landing. These early people made clearings in the woodland to plant crops and create the first farms, felling thousands of trees as they did so. In places like north Mayo, the wholesale destruction of the huge forest that ran along the coast created the blanket bog of today.

THE FIRST DOLMENS

Some time around 4000 BC Ireland's earliest farmers decided to honour the dead in a formalised way through the construction of tombs created from huge rocks left behind from Ice-Age boulder fields. At this time, farming and the subsequent rise in population numbers may have led to the need to differentiate between families. Archaeologists believe the same process was happening in Europe at that time, as family groups began to reuse the boulders in a startlingly new way.

The people of ancient Sligo started to build simple tripod dolmens, collecting three or more large and heavy squat boulders to form a base, then placing a capstone weighing five or six tons on top and finishing the exercise by creating a surrounding circle of smaller stones. It was a Herculean effort and made a big statement that these people were here to stay and were no longer inconsequential in nature's great scheme of things. The massive stone dolmens were markers in time, something that would last for ever.

Following page:
Creatures of the
Apocalypse from
the 9th century
Moone High Cross

A Stone-Age
symbol from Sliabh
na Cailleach in
County Meath

This period probably saw individual farming/hunting units aggregate into clans and the subsequent reorganisation of collectively owned or

managed territory into boundaried land, defined by walls, and, more importantly, ancestral tombs. Ownership and fecundity of the tribal land was related in an intimate way to the tombs and what they represented. At the Ceide Fields in north Mayo, elaborate stone field boundaries from 5,000 years ago suggest both the corralling of cattle and the intended inheritance of land. But ecology was not understood. The open moorland and bogs of Mayo are a result of things that are still happening today across the world. Thousands of years ago, the clearance of woodland resulted in the washing away of topsoil and the resultant rise in the water table, leaving early farmers with no choice but to move on and slash more forest. The bog enveloped the homesteads of those farmers.

Yet one of the questions about those distant times, perhaps before climatic decline, must be what they thought about, after food, shelter and other human needs. In times of plenty, did they ponder the mysteries of their surroundings any more than we do? Or did they just get on with their lives, content to work and to live. The society that created the tombs of the Boyne Valley expended huge amounts of time and effort building the passage tombs and then decorating the internal and external surfaces with elaborate designs that held significance for them. These farmer-astronomers had moved beyond subsistence and were using their surplus

labour to create monuments and instruments of observation. Their stone 'art' may relate to solar and lunar movements, or be more symbolic, possibly due to their understanding of a solar god or gods and their powers and spheres of influence.

Following page:
Ripening barley, an
essential crop of
the ancient past
fills the sky in
Carlow

But perhaps the carvings preceded the tombs in some other form, in that the shapes and circles may have already been part of their magical understanding of the world. One theory is that the symbols on the inside of the tombs represented the souls of the tribe, so a newborn baby had no 'soul' until one of the tribal ancestors inhabited its body. Conceivably, places like Newgrange were repositories of the tribal spirits and each new infant was somehow an incarnation of one of the deceased of the tomb. A new baby was 'baptised' into the tribe through ritual in the darkness.

In Melanesia in the Pacific, stone tripod structures like Irish dolmens have a special meaning: 'to come out from, to be born'. To the Pacific Islanders, the dolmen symbolises 'a cave through which the dead must pass on their journey to the other world and a womb through which the living may achieve rebirth'.

WEATHER AS DESTINY

If we could talk to an Irish person of 4,000 years ago, we would recognise situations that sound familiar, yet strange from that distant context. For example, people worry today about global warming, but overnight climate collapse in an agrarian society had far more catastrophic effects. You cannot grow without heat. After a year your stock is gone. Likewise, if my sky is lit at night by gods hurling thunderbolts that burn the very air, scorch the ground, I would quake in terror before such awesome power. And I might change my beliefs. The evidence for such ideas lies under a bog in Offaly and a deep glacier ice-core. Climate change happened not once but several times over the last few thousand years and profoundly affected the way people on this island thought about everything they knew. And an entirely new form of thinking may have emerged when the climate changed negatively as a result of an astronomical event. Evidence suggests that major asteroid phenomena altered the skies of Ireland several times over the last 7,000 years, with serious results in at least one case when the climate rapidly changed. When a major celestial event occurred, things

A sky-gazing pre-Christian
idol in a corner of Armagh's
Church of Ireland cathedral

often got cold very quickly, causing people to question their beliefs especially if the warming effect of spring and summer sunshine failed. It would challenge whether or not their gods were any good in the face of this outside threat. If not, let's follow the stronger god.

These climate-caused ideological shifts link together over time to form a chain from past to present. Coincidence in the ancient past becomes providence as people adapt and alter their tribal history-story. A new mythology of the ancient world emerges, of gods striking gods in a great contest in the sky until one triumphs and the skies clear again. There is a new god. Now we must develop a new way of worship, different to the old way. Chance creates new paradigms.

A decorative panel from the broken cross at Kells seems to represent the swirling weather patterns of cyclones and anti-cyclones

An Irish king and family representing Noah on the Ark await the tide in their timber-built 'cog', a cross-channel transport boat of Medieval Ireland. From the Book of Ballymote in the library of the Royal Irish Academy

TRADE BEGINS

Trade had begun even in that early time. Scotland had little flint or hard stone for axe heads, while County Antrim had plenty. Business appears to have been brisk across the North Channel and axe heads of Antrim porcellanite are found in many locations in western Scotland. The connection between Scotland and Antrim created a society that shared a common culture and language and for millennia had its own dynamic of shared customs and politics. Certainly by the Roman period, merchants bringing wine from the Mediterranean came to know knew the ports of Ireland. It was a prolific foundry in the Bronze Age, producing copper axes, swords and bronze halberds (a sythe on a pole), which are superb examples of the metalworkers' art. This period is often referred to as Ireland's first Golden Age, as the ruling elite commissioned elegant gold torcs and lunulae, a form of rigid gold necklace, as indicators of wealth or special status. Over time, merchants sailed both west and east of Ireland on their route north and came to know what Ireland had to offer. Ships from Gaul knew the south in the time of Caesar, and oil and wine were exchanged with the merchants and nobility of Ireland from early times.

As the country evolved in trade, the Irish elite developed contacts in continental Europe, and art styles and ideas became reflected in the work produced. The gold collection of the National Museum is one of the largest pre-historic collections in Europe and it

A gold torc and dress-fastner from the the Bronze Age of c.2500 years ago. Pictures courtesy of the National Museum of Ireland

A replica Bronze-Age urn from the Kerry County museum collection

35

represents, to this writer at least, the imaginative picture many people have of Celtic Ireland. The actual remains from the Iron Age or Celtic period are slim by comparison.

Bronze Age Ireland was a wealthy society, exploiting the seams of copper ore in places like Ross Island near Killarney and the Beara Peninsula. Some mines still exist, eerie shafts that decline into the hill before disappearing under water. Slag heaps of discarded rock and scorched stone from the technique of heating the ore bearing seams are still to be seen. Not all our tribal ancestors were eco-friendly and the wholesale clearing of the forests of Kerry and west Cork happened 3,000 years ago, because miners needed the fire to open the copper seams of the mountains. Like today, the energy demands of industry created wealth but problems as well. The timber of Munster was first stripped to fire the Bronze Age furnaces.

Traders exchanged amber from the Baltic for cattle hides, wolf-dogs and sometimes hawks. Ireland's position on an ancient sailing route is a key to understanding how cultural influences travel backwards and forwards across water and sometimes their artefacts and social impact last

Warriors on horseback with shields and weapons parade across the base of the Kells market cross

36

across time itself. Being an island on a major maritime route was Ireland's gain.

Gradually the Irish began to develop agriculture, the knowledge being partly their own and partly new expertise acquired through transfer systems whereby, excess cattle hides, pottery, bone and antler jewellery were exchanged for salt, weapons and perhaps people.

As farming skills increased, so did population and some people became specialised within the group, becoming Shamans, an early form of Druid. Most of these early societies had highly developed ideas about the gods.

Most archaeologists agree that women were at the forefront of several things that truly changed the world. The domestication of animals and the cultivation of grain crops probably began with women somewhere in the area known as the Fertile Crescent, where the Tigris and the Euphrates create a sweep of irrigated and fertile land, which supported a rising civilisation over 6,000 years ago.

Women may have begun the process of refining wild grass seed into different species, creating what became the great food crops of the world.

The goddess of Fourknocks tomb in County Meath guards the mysteries of the Stone-Age

By sorting wild grass seed, grain such as barley was created. Across Europe, similar things were taking place and gradually communities began to grow sufficient food to meet their needs and thereby allow a society and a modest civilisation to develop.

Ireland's first Megalithic tombs and associated rock art coincide with the introduction of agriculture at the beginning of the Neolithic or New Stone Age (4000 – 2400 BC). Only after our pre-historic ancestors were able to settle in a particular area and produce their own staple diet did it make sense to erect burial monuments. It was the consequence of an improved standard of living, one with enhanced resources.

Bronze-Age ceramics from Mount Dalton in County Westmeath and the Kerry County Museum, Tralee

NEOLITHIC INNOVATIONS: POTTERY

Ireland's Mesolithic hunters and gatherers first used containers made from easily available materials such as wood and leather, but then somebody, again probably female, made a real discovery. By heating the right type of clay and drying out the water, they could induce a chemical change in the hydrated aluminium that is the principal component of clay. Now they could make pottery. Those who invented the technique probably used their own hair to make the braiding, which decorated the pottery vessel. Local and regional variations in style developed across Ireland.

In many Megalithic tombs, great quantities of broken pottery have been found, suggesting that the breaking of pots, perhaps containing the ashes of the deceased, was part of the burial rite. If the pots contained a liquid such as beer, the splashing of the liquid may have symbolised a baptism of some form, the pouring liquid representing rebirth.

Some pots have been found intact, suggesting they may have had domestic use as soup-bowls, or mugs. Examples of this pottery have been found across the North Channel at several Scottish sites, but with a simpler form of decoration, suggesting gradual development as the 'potters' moved eastwards to Scotland and back again to Ireland. Examples of similar pottery from the Isle of Man show how the potters used bird-bones for making decorations on their pots, employing the open end of the quill and ball-and-knuckle joints to impress the wet clay.

One type of pottery with crude external decorations incised into the clay with sticks or bird-bones is called Carrowkeel Ware, found essentially in passage tombs. Unlike today, pottery vessels were not mere domestic objects, but many were imbued with ritual properties during that Bronze Age when pots containing cremated bone were common burial deposits.

But they were not a blind-faith people. As well as being associated with ritual, magic or worship, their structures of dolmens and passage tombs were firstly exercises in imagination, the beginnings of metaphysics, a three-dimensional speculation in philosophy, reaching into space and time, using the power of imagination, the greatest tool we possess as humans. They saw the heavens above as a thing of beauty, perfection in the sky that could be attempted only second-hand as it were, in their medium of stone. Art to them may have been a religious interpretation of the stars, expressed in two-dimensions on a slab of granite.

The art that decorates the tombs of the Boyne shows that the builders and designers had a sophisticated understanding of planetary movement and solar and lunar cycles. They created a hierarchical society based on agriculture, yet when climate change occurred, they adapted and survived. But their art and tombs were abandoned as a new type of community worship emerged.

3 MEGALITHIC TOMBS

IRELAND'S NEOLITHIC FARMERS were the first to create long-lasting stone monuments – Megalithic tombs and Megalithic cemeteries. The word megalith is derived from two Greek words, *mega* and *lithos*, meaning great stone. These tombs are burial chambers built of large stones, many of which were originally covered with a cairn of smaller stones or a mound of earth; the burial chambers reached through a narrow entrance. After thousands of years the large unhewn stones creating the chamber are often all that is left of the original tomb.

Haroldstown Dolmen [Portal omb] in Co.Carlow

There are still over 1,500 known tombs in Ireland. The majority of these date to the Neolithic period (4000–2400 BC) with the exception of Wedge tombs (see following page), which date mainly to the Early Bronze Age (2400–2000 BC). Most Megalithic tombs can be classified into several major types, each named after their distinctive shapes and features:

This is a brief summary of the major types.

PORTAL TOMBS

The ubiquitous 'Dolmen', often a tripod of stone with a chamber beneath a larger roof slab, weighing sometimes in excess of twenty tons.

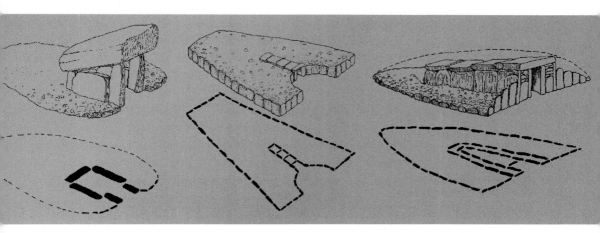

assage tombs – Oval tombs with a hamber often at the end of a long assage

Court tombs – Long mounds with an oval forecourt

Wedge tombs – Tomb with a wedge-shaped chamber but no interior passage

The earliest tombs in Ireland – but this is controversial – were simple stone tripods with a heavier stone as a roof. They are widely distributed and date from the Neolithic age, a time when farming was beginning. Perhaps the rapid cycle of generations was deemed to be too ephemeral, and stone summarised the effort of clearing the forests, a task involving immense time and labour.

These dolmens, which occur across Ireland, show the first imaginings of an agrarian people, moving beyond the merely functional into the metaphysical, where things can mean more than their utilitarian and surface

Knockeen Portal Tomb in Co. Waterford has a unique 'keyhole' entrance, perhaps to offer food to the spirits of the dead, or allow cult members access

appearance. The dolmens were an early type of religious building, a space dedicated to the rituals of birth and death. Perhaps all religious thought circles those great issues and comes to some interpretation that suits the believers.

It was originally thought that each tomb type preceded another, so that as the builders became more skilful, they built and designed more complicated structures. Another complementary theory is that as new arrivals landed in Ireland from the Baltic or Iberia, Brittany, they brought a new technique with them, so that their tombs reflected the burial types and rites of their homeland.

Most Court, Passage and Portal tombs are in the north and north east of Ireland. In the tombs of the Boyne Valley, as yet only Passage tombs have been

One of the many tombs at Carrowmore, in Co.Sligo

discovered. Passage tombs are sometimes grouped together to create Megalithic cemeteries, as at the Boyne Valley or on hilltops such as Lough-crew, Co. Meath.

Now, however, many archaeologists believe that the different types of tombs may be distinct status objects, suggesting a hierarchical society differentiating itself through the deployment of elaborate symbolic objects in the landscape. In other words, my tomb is bigger, or at least different from your tomb.

In Carrowmore, in the west of Ireland, close to the rich mussel beds of Sligo Bay, lies a city of the dead. Over one hundred tombs may have once stood in a vast complex of temples, ritual stone circles and burial mounds.

The Portal Tomb of Ballina, Co. Mayo

CARROWMORE

This extraordinary site is the largest Megalithic cemetery in Europe, with almost 60 remaining tombs scattered across a number of fields and alongside modern roads. Many of the tombs have been damaged through their reuse for field-boundaries, but a sufficient number remain to

give a sense of the immense importance the site had for the people of some 5,000 years ago. They were among the first farmers in Ireland and probably cleared the elm forests that existed around Carrowmore at that time.

The tombs form a carefully constructed ritual landscape, built by those people of long ago to form a sacred space, wherein ancestors were venerated and the dead cremated and placed inside to join them.

The glacial boulders scattered across the Knocknarea Peninsula in County Sligo were made into over 100 tombs and arranged around a huge oval at Carrowmore where the last, Listoghil was built. The people exploited the rich inshore fishing grounds and may have had intense contacts with other Atlantic coastal groups. The tombs may represent different clans or be symbols of dominant elites who had come to power.

According to standard archaeology, simple passage tombs such as those at Carrowmore date to around 3500 BC, so they are roughly five and a half millennia old. The dates have been found through carbon-14 dating and are becoming generally accepted. Swedish archaeological excavations at Carrowmore revealed, however, remarkably earlier dates. Three tombs, numbers 4, 7 and 27, produced dateable material, that placed Carrowmore among the earliest Megalithic cemeteries in Europe. One of the archaeologists who undertook the excavations is Stefan Bergh from National University of Ireland, Galway, who has studied the passage tombs of Sligo for more than 20 years.

From one particular tomb we got two dates from about 7,000 years ago (5000 BC) which seems to indicate that some kind of activity was going on here at a very early stage. The Carrowmore tombs are fairly simple tombs. They could easily have been built by an extended family and this might be the reason why we have such a large number of tombs here. Sixty tombs survive today but originally there might have been as many as one hundred.

The dead would have been placed on the floor of the chamber. We do not know for sure the precise number of individuals but as the dead were cremated it would have been possible to fit a lot of people into a chamber like this. Not everybody would have been buried in these tombs; probably only a few were selected. We simply do not know how people were selected. It could have been the seventh son or everybody with red hair and a limp.

The dates produced suggested a usage of the site from 5000 BC, a surprising fifteen centuries earlier than had previously been assumed. Dates as early as this, however, have been found in other tombs in pre-historic Europe, such as Barnenez and Ite Guennoc in Brittany and Cha de Parada in Galicia. In another tomb in the coastal region of Loire-Atlantique, flint tools have been found in a passage grave, a type of tomb with a long passage to the burials in the centre, similar to Newgrange, Knowth and Dowth. Could the dates prove that Ireland's tomb-building tradition started in Carrowmore as early as on the Continent? This is still debated by many archaeologists in Ireland. Only further discovery of dateable material can end the controversy. For Stefan Bergh, the problem with these early dates lies with the flaws inherent in the dating process:

> Radiocarbon dating is notoriously inaccurate – you need dozens of similar results to be sure of an age. The problem is that we only have two other comparable dates. To me the exact age is not all that important. The important task is to establish how these tombs relate to other tombs that were built in Ireland. Which ones came first? Another interesting question is why the people who lived at Carrowmore constructed these tombs. They are not designed to impress or be seen from far away. That tells us something about the people who built them because you don't need to erect stone tombs to dispose of dead relatives – there are much easier ways of doing that. The fact, however, that they did, tells us about a completely new way of honouring or remembering the dead. These buildings are a statement – they show that ritual played an important part when it comes to disposing of the dead. For the first time ever these tombs created a sacred space. They were monuments to the ancestors and places of worship. I think the Carrowmore tombs can be compared to a family parish church. A new religion was coming.
>
> Stefan Bergh, *Department of Archaeology, NUI Galway*

The ancient community that created the Carrowmore tombs was not a static one, and society changes – willingly or not. By looking at the different building stages and the arrangement and sequence of monuments, such changes in society might still be discernible.

The tombs of Carrowmore are built of circular patterns of large glacial boulders with a dolmen in the centre. Most tombs are arranged to face inwards towards the focal point of the cemetery, the western tombs facing east and the eastern facing west. The landscape is dominated by the massive tomb of Queen Maeve, a cairn that sits atop the mountain of Knocknarea. The placing of the cairn in such a highly visible location signifies the elevation of the ancestors into the sky, the raising-up of the dead towards the heavens. It also suggests a rising sense of ownership among the community, using the bones of the dead as a 'signpost' of identity, so that anyone approaching the area around Sligo could see who owned this land, the property of a community.

LISTOGHIL

The centre of the 'City of the Dead' is Listoghil, tomb 51, a new departure in Megalithic monument-building. It began as an uncovered tomb like the rest, but was covered in to create a cairn, or mound of stones that conceals the tomb. It was also the very last tomb to be built at Carrowmore around 5,500 years ago. Stefan Burgh says:

> Listoghil is the largest tomb at Carrowmore and its construction marked the start of a new trend of monument building. It features a massive roof-slab of limestone weighing about seven to eight tons. The roof-slab probably originated from the northern slopes of Knocknarea, about six or seven kilometres from Carrowmore. Instead of resting on five orthostats [upright stones] like the surrounding tombs, Listoghil rests on six. They were placed in a rectangle, hence creating a rectangular chamber. In between the orthostats and the roof-slab are smaller sandstone slabs which were probably part of the construction as well. The orthostat at the front of Listoghil, remarkably, does not support the roof-slab, which indicates that it might have been part of a construction that predates the building of the actual chamber. When this chamber was constructed, it was built as a free-standing chamber, the way we can still see it today. A new development, however, was that at some stage, perhaps after ten or even fifty years, the entire chamber was sealed under a massive cairn, a large pile of smaller stones. This was a major statement since it was the first time that our

ancestors covered their tombs with cairns. It tells us is that the presence of monuments in the landscape became increasingly important. Cairns became larger, some of them huge, and they were built in more conspicuous places. It indicates a new way of thinking and a new way of dealing with your ancestors.

What makes Listoghil so important is the fact that it differs considerably from other tombs within the cemetery in both size and construction. It is located in the middle of the oval cluster of all the other tombs. Archaeologists think that Listoghil is crucial to our understanding of the function and symbolism of the ritual landscape of Carrowmore cemetery. Even though Listoghil was the last and most important of the tombs built there, it represents only a stage in the development of the Mesolithic building

Listoghil, tomb 51 became the focal point of the Carrowmore complex and may represent both the beginnings of megalithic art in Ireland and the start of Cairn building.
19th century antiquarians recorded finding bones of horses and stone arrowheads in its interior

tradition in County Sligo. The next monument our ancestors built was Queen Maeve's tomb on Knocknarea – Ireland's most visually dominating Neolithic monument. It is twice the size of Listoghil. Stefan Burgh explains:

40,000 metric tons of limestone cover Maeve's Tomb on Knocknarea, Co Sligo. The queen, possibly a real figure from the Iron-Age is by tradition buried upright in the tomb, facing her enemies in Ulster

'Listoghil needed to be big because it was trying to influence people from all around the Carrowmore area. The problem is – it's built on a plateau. To reach a wider audience, the architects had to build higher up. They built Queen Maeve's tomb. By building this monument our ancestors transformed the entire mountain into a site of worship.'

Maeve's Cairn, a 55m (180ft) diameter cairn is the reputed burial place of Queen Maeve of Connacht, thought to have ruled the west of Ireland in the first century AD. She was, in the words of W.B. Yeats, *'queen of the invisible host, who sleeps high up on Knocknarea, in an old cairn of stones'*.

CARROWKEEL - MEGALITHIC CEMETERY

Just 20 kilometres south of Carrowmore lies another group of fourteen passage tombs at Carrowkeel in the Bricklieve Mountains. Some archaeologists think of Carrowmore and Carrowkeel as two related Megalithic cemeteries, yet it is also plausible to view them as a vast unified ritual landscape. The passages of most of the Carrowkeel tombs are pointing towards the Cúil Irra peninsula of Sligo and hence towards the Megalithic cemetery at Carrowmore and Miosgán Medhbha – Queen Maeve's tomb. This tomb was very likely the ritual focus of the Megalithic landscape. It is clearly visible from the Carrowkeel monuments.

Frank Prendergast from the School of Archaeology at University College Dublin has explored the relationship between the passage tombs of Ireland and the astronomy and astrological beliefs of their builders.

These stone tombs were far more than burial mounds – they were central places within the tribal landscape – places that symbolised the importance of the tribal area. They advertised the tribe's domain to anyone and everyone. These huge, labour-costly monuments and their suburban satellites were, like the Egyptian pyramids, built to impress and dominate all who saw them and no doubt they guaranteed a favourable position in the afterlife. By putting tombs on high ground, you are in a sense connecting those tombs with the power of the mountain itself. They were imbued with symbolic meaning for a variety of reasons, not all of which we can ever understand because there was no manual; there is no blueprint and we have to try and interpret from the evidence that remains what was in the mind of the builders at that time.

One of the least known of Ireland's ancient sites, Carrowkeel is a large group of passage tombs situated on the upper slopes of the Bricklieve Mountains in Co. Sligo. Excavations dated the tombs to 3340BC and they were used for several thousand years, perhaps as the entrance to the underworld

Carrowkeel was designed to be seen from the north only – from Carrowmore. If you were looking from the south, you wouldn't even know it was here. They also tell us about an important development. They require huge labour resources and must have been built by a fairly well-organised society. These were no longer common farmers – they were a structured, governed society obsessed with astronomy and astrology. These tombs on the west coast of Ireland are classic examples of the simpler passage grave form. As we move towards the east of the island, it's apparent that the size of the tombs and the sophistication and complexity of the tombs are increasing.

Civilisation in fact is moving forward; it is evolving and ideas are perhaps being experimented with. It may be sparked locally or it could be new ideas coming in from elsewhere. But whatever the motivation, significant change is happening.

Frank Prendergast, *Dublin Institute of Technology*

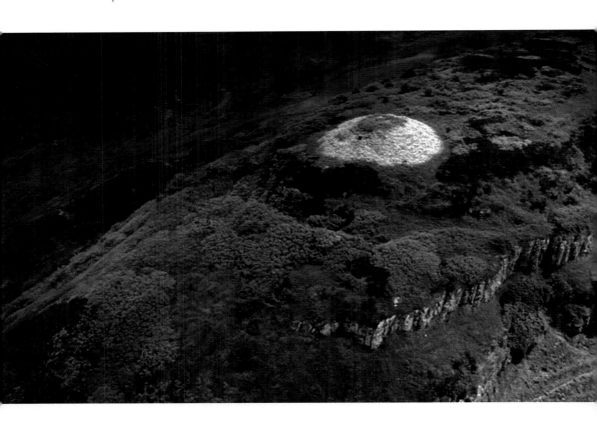

THE TOMBS OF THE BOYNE VALLEY

IRELAND'S PYRAMIDS

4

THE PEOPLE WHO constructed the tombs of Sligo and the Boyne valley may have had beliefs in common. If you were a Neolithic farmer, your deities surrounded you; they were in the stones, the earth and the stars, and to a great degree, they were real, not imaginary. The tombs perhaps were some three-dimensional representation of an aspect of that god, growing out of the earth, rounded and womb-like, as if they are repositories of some 'mana' or spiritual substance, reservoirs of tribal ancestors perhaps. In the days before intra-uterine medicine, conception was not fully understood and becoming pregnant may have had further meaning for our ancestors. In other early societies that continued into the twentieth century, people believed that souls were limited in number and that pregnancy would not lead to a successful birth unless the pregnant woman spent time in a special place where the souls of the ancients were kept. Perhaps the tombs of the Boyne Valley were a 'soul bank' that retained the spirits of the departed, and a woman hoping to conceive a son or daughter who would become a warrior or a wizard, or even just be healthy, would spend a night in the tomb hoping for a favourable *ensoulment*.

Some tombs have legends that turn out to be true. *Cailleach* is a word often used to describe the Hag aspect of the female, a withering and

malevolent 'witch'. It was also used to describe nuns, as in Calliaghstown, a medieval nunnery in County Westmeath. In Cork, an ancient tradition had named a burial mound as *Leaba na Cailleach*, 'the bed of the witch', and, while it is generally understood that no oral tale can survive more than five hundred years, when excavated in the 1930s the wedge-shaped tomb contained, amongst other bones, a single skeleton and separated head of a woman, perhaps of high status, buried 3,000 years before.

In a later period, the mythological tale of Dechitre, a mother-goddess in human form, after having a child die, is seduced by the great god Lugh, in Newgrange and, after aborting the child because of accusations of incest, has the same child again. This time the child is Setanta, a triple-born god,

Leaba na Cailleagh, the Bed of the Witch, near Fermoy, Co. Cork, whose legend survived in Gaelic folklore

54

similar to many triple deities around the time of Roman Britain. It may be the case that incoming Celtic tribes wishing to place themselves in already existing tribal narratives rewrote the stories with themselves included, or rather put a chosen ancestor into the tale which showed him being reborn within the older society.

The tombs of the Boyne valley are probably Ireland's most important early buildings. They qualify as 'buildings' because they were designed and constructed with a complex understanding of weight, mass, gravity and permanence. Even weather and rain penetration were understood and allowed for.

But the tombs of the Boyne valley also have a scientific basis. Few would disagree that they were used to observe natural phenomena. They appear capable of marking the rotation of the galaxies, the passage of the moon across the heavens and the yearly calendar by way of the sun's entry into the inner chamber of Newgrange on 21 December, the winter solstice. Given that the people who built these tombs were farmers, more inclined to animal management and crop husbandry, their technical achievement is spectacular.

Perhaps the tombs also had a philosophical function. In the Stone Age,

The mysterious mound of Dowth awaits scientific excavation

seasons, animals, generations passed year by year and little was left to mark their existence. If you construct a great monument, however, it leaves your signature upon the earth for all time. Your name will live on. Because the people of the Boyne Valley were illiterate, we have no way of knowing anything of their beliefs and certainly not their names or politics. But we can surmise that they were organised in large enough numbers to create such immense buildings. Whether they acted collectively with consent or by coercion we cannot say, but one imagines that a little force would go a long way in getting these tombs built. A trans-generational building programme that involved the quarrying and transportation of thousands of tons of granite, plus the elaborate layering of gravels and shales to form the body of the tombs required a large workforce. The feeding, housing and organisation of such a large group required an administrative staff, so perhaps the building of the tombs eventually created an elite that became its priests. In Egypt, the building of the Pyramids created a 'middle-class' of clerics dedicated to the rituals and functions of the buildings. Perhaps Ireland's 'Valley of the Kings' was the same.

The custom of building Megalithic tombs did not originate in Ireland. It spread across Neolithic Europe and reached this island around 6,000 years ago. Megalithic graves dating from 5000 BC to 3000 BC are scattered thorough Spain, Portugal, Ireland, Britain and the Scandinavian countries.

Some experts believe the earliest form is the 'Court Cairn' or lobster cairn, so-called because of its enclosing forecourt 'arms'. These date from around 4000 BC and often involve a most elaborate system of interior interconnected chambers with the exterior forecourt used for ritual or cremation. In the interior chambers were placed the bones or cremated remains of the tribes' male and female members. We have no way of knowing who got buried in such tombs, and the chance of being buried in this way may have involved a lottery, family ties, dynastic privilege or human sacrifice.

NEWGRANGE, KNOWTH AND DOWTH

The builders of Ireland's most famous passage tombs – those of Newgrange, Knowth and Dowth – were not Celtic as we understand the term, but their enigmatic rock art of spirals, whorls and lozenges has been incorporated into the canon of 'Celtic Art'. Their ancient

Opposite page: A fragment of a Gaelic astronomical *Rotula* with a moveable index showing the planets and signs of the zodiac. It was based on the writings of Masha'llah Ibn Ahari, a Persian astrologer who died in 815 AD. The manuscript was also a medical textbook, but many if its pages were later cut into heart-shaped amulets, probably to protect against a plague.

Library of the Royal Irish Academy

Gaelic scholars
kept the legends of
Newgrange alive
and the tales
speak of future
kings spending
time in the
darkness and
heroes being
revived within its
sanctuary

structures have become part of the Celtic narrative, appearing in later myth and legend as being the place of entrance to the underworld and the residence of the Sidhe, the unseen people of the underworld.

The Boyne Valley area predates the great Pyramids of Egypt by over a thousand years. Yet clearly the ritual part of the landscape was set out with sophistication and a knowledge of science and astronomy.

Frank Prendergast *School of Archaeology, University College Dublin*

Newgrange was well known within the written Gaelic tradition, but it culturally disappeared when a new elite came to power and the Irish language declined. By an irony of history, the land upon which Newgrange stood was part of the confiscated lordship of Mellifont abbey.

Dowth is part of a series of three giant tombs and other ritual enclosures within the bend of the Boyne river between Drogheda and Slane. It is located just less than two kilometres north-east of Newgrange. There are two tombs in the western part of the mound, dating from about 3000 BC. As at the other two great mounds, many of Dowth's kerbstones and interior stones bear Megalithic art, albeit not as sophisticated as the sister tombs. Newgrange, the largest of the three mounds, was not rediscovered until 1699. Together with the neighbouring tombs at Knowth and Dowth, it forms a Megalithic necropolis of international importance.

There have been no excavations at Dowth since 1847, but excavations at Newgrange and the main mound at Knowth produced a series of radiocarbon dates, placing them in the latter part of the fourth millenium BC 3500 – 3000 BC.

In Ireland there may be around 300 passage tombs, yet Knowth has more carved stones than all others combined. Knowth contains twenty-five percent of the megalithic art of western Europe and twice as many decorated stones as the entire Iberian peninsula

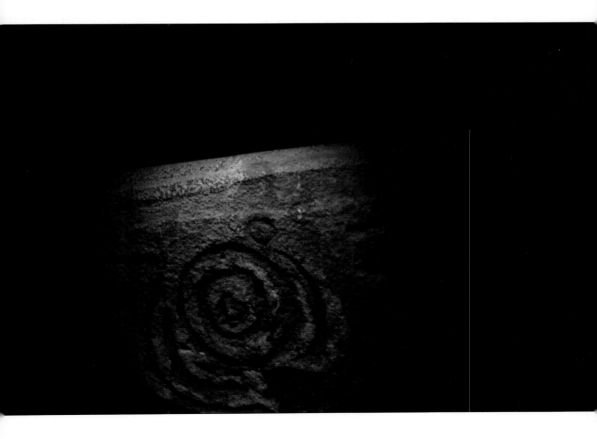

59

Knowth is a very substantial art gallery with over 300 stones. Well, we can call it art but probably a correct term for it is religious symbolism. It is associated with the cult of the dead and indeed it was the dead and the burial that occasioned the construction and the building of these outstanding structures. When we started excavating at Knowth in 1962 there was evidence for one or possibly two tombs. This number has been increased by twenty!

George Eogan, *UCD, Department of Archaeology*

Picture by Joe Fenwick

The great mound at Knowth (about 40 feet high and 220 feet in diameter) covers two passage tombs, which were discovered in the 1960s. The mound is surrounded by a kerb of 127 large stones, many of which are richly decorated, as is the inside of the tomb.

Professor George Eogan started excavations at Knowth in 1962. Forty years of digging revealed many surprising and exciting finds. The great mound is about nine metres high and covers an area of an acre and a half. On 11 July 1967 Eogan and his team discovered one of the longest passages in any known tomb. It measures more than 30 metres from the kerbstone to the back of the chamber.

I discovered a basin in the western chamber of Knowth. The preparation and creation of this granite basin alone was a very considerable work. The purpose of the basin was to hold the cremated remains and, of course, as the basin filled up there was quite a lot of cremation scattered over the floor of the recess as well as the basin.

George Eogan, *UCD, Department of Archaeology*

Following page:
A decorated Megalith from Gavrinis echoes Knowth and Newgrange

....
➤

Bones are the most frequent object recovered from the tombs and can look the same from generation to generation. Bones tell us about a person's health and diet and sometimes about how their life was ended with the blow of an axe. Noteworthy people only were buried in the tombs; a few had special jewellery suggesting they were either royalty or otherwise exceptional. They may even have died peacefully.

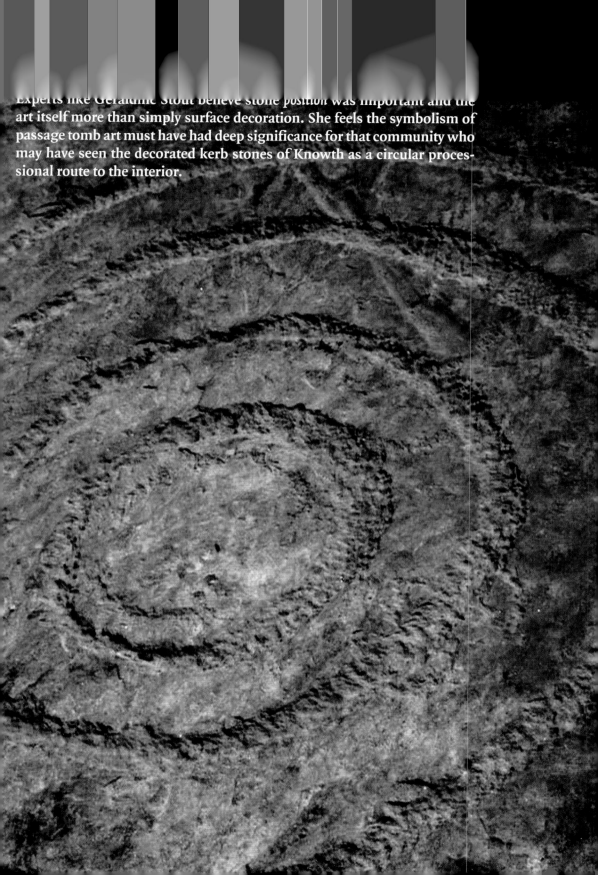

Experts like Geraldine Stout believe stone *position* was important and the art itself more than simply surface decoration. She feels the symbolism of passage tomb art must have had deep significance for that community who may have seen the decorated kerb stones of Knowth as a circular processional route to the interior.

ANALYSIS OF CREMATED REMAINS AT KNOWTH

We know little about the lives of our Neolithic ancestors who constructed Newgrange, Knowth and Dowth. The latest forensic techniques are being used to unlock the secrets of the dead of Knowth to reveal who they were, how they lived and how they died. Laureen Buckley, one of the leading osteo-archaeologists in Ireland is analysing the cremated remains excavated at Knowth, a painstaking scientific endeavour.

The bone analysis is far from complete, but already her work has proved that a considerable number of people, male and female, young and old, were interred in Knowth. Further work may reveal whether they were related or belonged to a single family or dynasty.

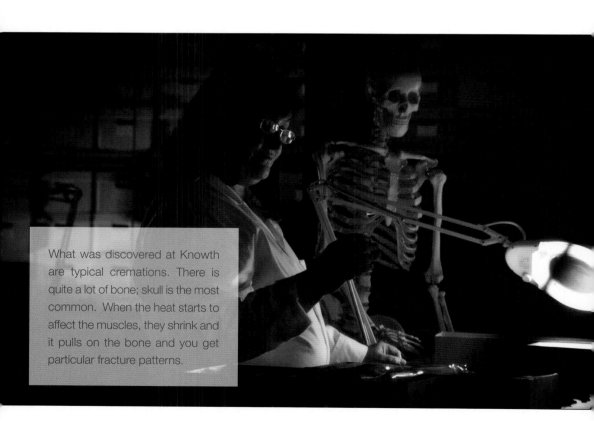

What was discovered at Knowth are typical cremations. There is quite a lot of bone; skull is the most common. When the heat starts to affect the muscles, they shrink and it pulls on the bone and you get particular fracture patterns.

The crystalline structure of it changes in the heat, so it actually becomes quite hard and this is why it lasts for thousands of years.

My job is to identify each piece and from that I can determine how many individuals were cremated and if they are adults or children. Some bone pieces appear polished. This is caused by osteoarthritis, which gets worse as we get older. There is also a a tiny piece of vertebra, belonging to an infant probably less than a year old. The next piece is a tooth. Teeth are also very important because they can tell us the age of the individual. I can tell that this particular tooth is from a baby of six months, so as well as the adult we have a baby among the cremated individuals. When I count the population of cremated remains, I expect nearly 100 individuals present.

Laureen Buckley, *Osteo-archaeologist*

A child's tooth
from over 4,000
years ago

◄

NEWGRANGE

Newgrange is the largest tomb of its type in Europe and one of the oldest. It is important also because of the orientation of its tomb passage to the rising sun of the winter solstice. Each year on 21 December,

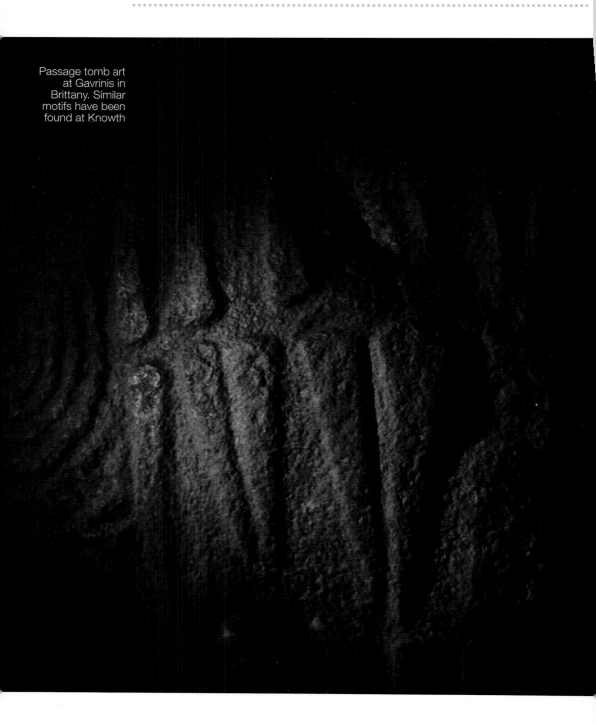

Passage tomb art at Gavrinis in Brittany. Similar motifs have been found at Knowth

the dawn sun shines through a 'roof box' illuminating the inner chamber, some 19m (62ft) inside the tomb. Although the equinox determined the seasonal action time of that community, the use of the roof box also established a space between Newgrange and the sun itself.

It may have functioned as a device for estimating time and space, by establishing a relationship between the physical world and the motions of the sun and stars. The roof box and subsequent observations suggested immense distance between the earth and objects in the sky, and that that distance and its relationship to movement could be measured and foreseen from year to year. It would have established the notions of past, present and future, which are all related to the concept of time and motion. In the observation of daylight entering the chamber on the winter solstice, the elite of the tribe would have witnessed the creation of time itself and a glimpse of the fleeting and unseizable nature of infinity.

Archaeologist Geraldine Stout examines the stones at Knowth

The stones at Dowth represent some of the earliest art in Ireland. You can see very crude circles; rayed features, zig-zag lines and each one of these designs would have had a powerful meaning for the society that carved them. What is remarkable is that we see some of these symbols throughout Europe. That suggests that these Neolithic communities had a shared religion. I think that the inspiration for this rock art came from Brittany in western France.

Geraldine Stout, *Archaeologist & Historian*

Passage tomb art
from Gavrinis,
Brittany

If you look at the rock art depicted at the passage tomb of Gavrinis, you can will see multiple arcs, spiral motifs, chevrons. It is so similar to the motifs at Dowth, it must have inspired the carvers there. If you look at the rock art at Knowth, you will see that one particular motif occurs again and again in the chamber in Gavrinis. This symbol is interpreted by the archaeologists there as the mother figure — a Neolithic idol. We can also see many of these curvilinear motifs which reflect the movement of the sun and the changes in the sun through the year. The decoration on one of the stones is very detailed and seems to represent a sundial. We have a hollow with a series of rays. And if this is a sundial, it emphasises their knowledge of astronomy. To me the similarity of rock art at Knowth, Dowth and Gavrinis is proof that the passage tomb builders of Ireland shared the same religion as the passage tomb builders in Brittany. Six thousand years ago the sea was the main form of transport for the people living along the coast. You can imagine missionaries full of their religious zeal and with the great knowledge of their passage tombs and their art and bringing that away with them to Ireland.

Geraldine Stout

The acceptance of the earth as being female, in its fecundity and nurturing aspect is fundamental to any understanding of the beliefs and perceptions of our prehistoric ancestors. Hills and valleys especially were seen as the dwelling place of the Great Earth Mother, Áine, *the smiling one*. In County Kerry, her twin mountains, the 'Breasts of Anu', retain their nipple-like cairns to this day. It seems natural that early farming communities would see the earth as essentially feminine, and respect this in symbol, thereby combining necropolis and sacred precinct. Since the earth was the matriarch who brought forth all living things, so earth mother as sacred structure seems appropriate for receiving the spirits of her children after death. Ireland's Megalithic tombs hence may have had several functions related to birth as well as death.

Creevy keel Court Cairn in Sligo, c.3500BC displays its complex interior after excavation

In the cycle of life, the goddess symbolised not only birth, fertility and life, she also was the bringer of death. She was a raptor, a winged ghost who took away the once-living flesh. Many Irish tombs seem to have an 'owl' type figure within the stone carving, a beaked bird of prey that may hark back to the burial process known as excarnation, where the flesh is stripped from the bones before burial.

Sliabh na Cailleach, the Hill of the Witch in County Meath, has over twenty-five

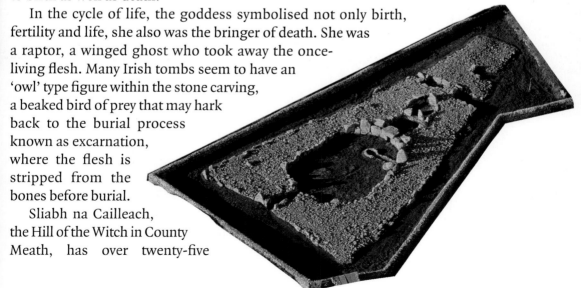

passage tombs, making it one of the largest passage-tomb cemeteries in Ireland. It lies in a landscape of many types of monuments and yet is almost an unexplored terrain. The area retains a curious sense of an older time, and the tombs have many forms of Megalithic art. The hills, like Tara to the southeast, formed part of an important ritual landscape of tombs, ritual approaches, standing stones and alignments. Finds included arrowheads, pottery, bone fragments and evidence of an art 'workshop' where later Celtic-type motifs were carved, as if to try out designs before using them on valuable metal.

History and archaeology have left Ireland richly endowed with monuments in every county. We take the term *monuments* for granted, as if those builders of antiquity intended it to be so. The word 'monuments' suggests an intention to leave something suitably impressive for succeeding generations, commemorating a past event or personage. In some cases this was true; an inscribed stone with cross and prayer is a true memorial to the deceased, but the earliest stone monuments, the dolmens or passage graves may not be memorials to any person in particular, but a family tomb, perhaps a marker to establish territory or a way of using the ancestors' bones to claim the land.

The ancient tombs hold many secrets awaiting discovery.

Opposite page: An interior stone at Sliabh na Caillighe [Hill of the Witch] in Co.Meath

One of the many beautifully decorated stones at Knowth.

I suspect about 3,200 years ago, a comet came close to this planet and showered the earth with its debris. But comet debris may not be small, you can get big chunks that form fire-balls. The largest chunks cause enormously violent explosions. People become terrified, because to them, the gods are angry and flinging thunderbolts from fiery chariots!

Professor Emeritus Mike Baillie,
*Dendrochronologist,
Queen's University Belfast*

An antennae of the Bronze-Age points towards Croagh Patrick, the holy mountain of County Mayo

5

FROM THE EARTH TO THE SKY

THE END OF THE TOMB BUILDING TRADITION IN IRELAND

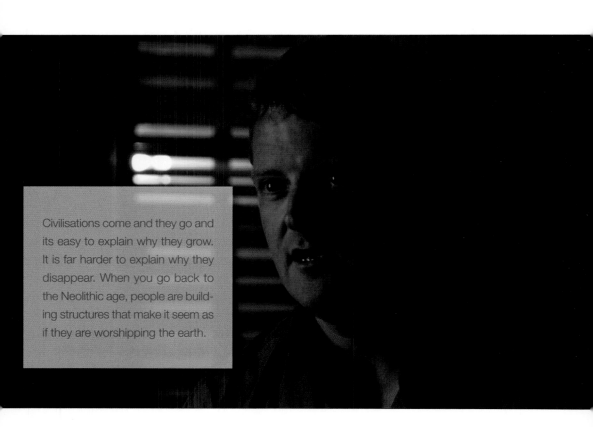

Civilisations come and they go and its easy to explain why they grow. It is far harder to explain why they disappear. When you go back to the Neolithic age, people are building structures that make it seem as if they are worshipping the earth.

Entering a passage tomb is like entering the earth effectively. It makes sense that Neolithic people, the first farmers, would worship the earth – the earth had been very good for them. If you come forward a bit, say 1,000 years or so, we have completely different structures — we have stone circles. Just think of Stonehenge as one of the biggest of these monuments. People stopped worshipping the earth and they started worshipping the sky. The question we have to ask is: Why did this huge change happen in the space of a thousand years?

Patrick McCafferty, *Queen's University Belfast and Armagh Observatory*

SIMILAR TO THE CHANGE that took place 6,000 years ago when agriculture was introduced to Ireland, several significant innovations took place in the period from 2500 – 2000 BC at the beginning of the Bronze Age. One of the most important innovations was the development of the craft of metalworking.

A replica Bronze-Age axe head from the Kerry County Museum

A particular type of tomb appeared during the Early Bronze Age called 'Wedge tombs'[See p.41] so named because they were wider at one end and canted at an angle. Wedge tombs represent the last phase of Ireland's Megalithic tomb tradition. They are the largest group of stone tombs in Ireland; more than 500 sites have so far been identified. This type of burial monument developed primarily in Munster and many were found near to ore-bearing deposits, while others were sited near a river, probably a boundary between tribes. Most held the bones of many generations, perhaps of the same mining, farming or territorial group.

In Bronze Age Ireland, many new types of burial site, stone circle and

standing stone appeared. These new monuments were completely different to the dark tombs of the preceding Stone Age. There was a significant change in burial practise and religious belief. Entirely new monuments appeared, testimony to important changes happening during that period.

A Wedge Tomb in west Cork, possibly built by Ireland's earliest miners and metal workers

THE EFFECTS OF CLIMATE CHANGE ON ANCIENT IRELAND

Today, climate change is seen as relatively new, man-made and potentially catastrophic. It is felt as a danger, something bigger than any one country, and it threatens the very existence of humankind. Rising temperatures are already having an effect worldwide in the increasing spread of deserts and a concurrent reduction in the productive capacity of less well-off nations. Floods threaten these low-lying and densely populated areas that have few resources to cope with such disasters.

New information about ancient climate change is showing how alterations in the temperature owing to volcanic eruption or comets colliding

Opposite page: The eye of the Owl Goddess on Sliabh na Cailleach in County Meath

75

The 12th century cathedral and Round Tower at Ardmore on a February morning

with the earth brought about major social upheaval because these natural occurrences were seen as supernatural events, the gods being angry or impotent in the face of new threats.

Unknown stories of Ireland's past are being revealed by new scientific techniques in archaeology. Long-established theory now has a chance of proof, and new evidence sheds light on dramatic changes in the earth's temperature, which may have fundamentally changed the way people lived their lives.

Momentous events in history and pre-history have altered societies suddenly, causing disruption to the established order and creating a new dynamic. We know that in the distant past rapid declines in the world climate caused major population movements and perhaps the breakdown of many societies. As temperatures dropped, crops failed, cattle starved, people died. There have been many periods in the last 5,000 years when Ireland experienced major climatic disruptions, and during the medieval period climatic decline resulted in crop failures and plague.

Society in the past has had periods like the twentieth century when change seemed to be sudden and violent, forcing long-held beliefs to be adapted or be forgotten. Significantly, carbon-dating of deep core samples from the arctic ice caps show climate change occurring around the time that significant social changes began in the past. It seems probable that spectacular natural events may have created at least one new religion and eased the passage of another.

When the event is significant enough, it transforms those involved, altering their understanding of the world and their place in it. An entirely new system sometimes emerges from such events, often powerful enough to be remembered far into the future, beyond the generation of direct experience. Sometimes what happened leaves a physical change in the landscape. For reasons not yet understood, the population group that lived in the Skyrne Valley of County Meath abandoned an immense timber temple on the Hill of Tara, the foundations of which lay undiscovered for over two millennia. Perhaps this was in response to climatic change or the deterioration of some aspect of their lives beyond which they could cope. The abandonment of the temple happened before legends began, and is not recorded in any ancient story or tale.

Climate change may alter the way we understand the world, and there are several examples of climate change affecting ancient Irish society in quite dramatic ways. Mike Baillie, Professor Emeritus of Palaeoecology at Queen's University Belfast has a fascinating theory as to why these great changes took place. Baillie is a leading expert in dendrochronology (dating by means of tree-rings). He was instrumental in establishing a year-by-year chronology of tree-ring growth reaching 7,400 years into the past.

When examining Ireland's dendrochronological record, Baillie noticed indications of severe environmental downturns around 2354 BC and again in 1628 BC, 1159 BC, 208 BC, and 540 AD. Evidence suggests that these environmental downturns were wide-ranging and catastrophic events, which seem to coincide with major changes in society such as the abandonment

Egyptian papyrus from the Bronze-Age refer to the 'Curse of Akkad', when the sun was veiled by dust for several years causing dramatic climate change and societal collapse

A fossilised 4,000 year old tree from a deep midlands bog shows a ring for every year of its age

of Newgrange-type tombs and the later adaptation of Christianity.

The first environmental downturn took place around 2400 BC at the end of the Stone Age and the beginning of the Bronze Age in Ireland. Could this really be a coincidence? Did the weather change society? Could a downturn in temperature be sufficient to alter beliefs? It seems the weather could be like a solvent, dissolving long-held beliefs and customs.

A tree ring record is the record produced by a tree during its lifetime – it is like a fingerprint. Although this oak looks to be in extremely good condition ,it was growing almost 4,500 years ago. You can see in this tree that the tree was putting on wide rings during its youth; suddenly it came to this point in time and you have a catastrophically bad set of growth rings – the tree was essentially putting on no summer wood at all. It was just managing to stay alive for about eighteen years. We can also tell from the tree-ring work that the last wide ring is 1160BC and the first of the really narrow rings is 1159BC. Around this time, the 12th century BC, you have the fall of Troy, the collapse of Greek civilization and a major dynastic change in China!

The tall Punchestown standing stone erected over a warrior burial over 3000 years ago

▼

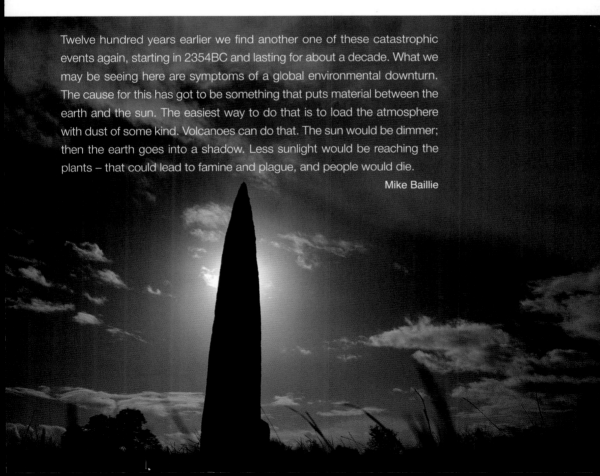

Twelve hundred years earlier we find another one of these catastrophic events again, starting in 2354BC and lasting for about a decade. What we may be seeing here are symptoms of a global environmental downturn. The cause for this has got to be something that puts material between the earth and the sun. The easiest way to do that is to load the atmosphere with dust of some kind. Volcanoes can do that. The sun would be dimmer; then the earth goes into a shadow. Less sunlight would be reaching the plants – that could lead to famine and plague, and people would die.

Mike Baillie

The problem with this theory is that volcanoes by and large have effects only for a few years. The catastrophic event in the 12th century BC lasted a lot longer, for about 18 years. Whatever caused the global environmental downturn must have dumped material a lot higher into the atmosphere. Comets can do that! If a comet deposits dust, it leaves it much higher up and the effects last for up to a decade or longer. What I suspect is that a comet came close to the earth and showered the earth with its debris. Comet debris is not just dust size; you can get larger chunks and these form fire balls. You can even get larger chunks and they cause enormously violent explosions. People start to be really afraid because the gods are throwing thunderbolts. As a result, they would have blamed the object in the sky. Once you start contemplating such issues, it has implications for what people might have believed. It allows you to think of concepts like the old gods not working and the new gods picking up where the old gods failed. Hence you might expect to see some kind of new religious outlook. If this object in the sky has such an effect on the people below, then it is enough reason to stop worshipping the earth and to start celebrating the sky, praying that they will survive that night. I think that would have been enough for people to switch their allegiance. They now were trying to appease the sky gods, starting to worship them, building monuments to them.

Mike Baillie, *Professor Emeritus of Palaeoecology, Queen's University Belfast*

In the past, if something as essential as the sun declined in power and crops stopped flourishing, it may have been thought that the sun god was dying or angry with the tribe. There is considerable evidence to suggest that catastrophic solar or cosmic events in the distant past may have triggered major social change; in the same way, many predict that climate change could radically affect western society. The difference with the past is that some of these events may have happened in a very short time, even within a year.

The comet, named 'Hale-Bopp' from the astronomers who discovered it, orbited the earth in 1997 on a return journey, and thousands watched its arc across the northern and southern hemispheres. It first appeared to the people of the Bronze Age over 4,000 years ago and may have been the cause of fundamental changes, if not widespread destruction, in several advanced societies. The comet originated in the constellation of stars known as Sagit-

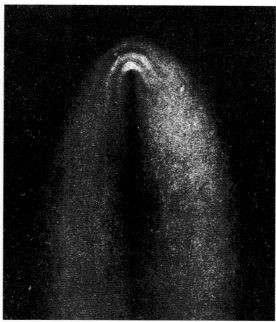

tarius and was possibly as large as 80 kilometres in diameter. It would have been observable over many months and with a glowing tail 50,000,000 kilometres long would have presented a frightening sight in the sky. The early civilisations of Egypt and Mesopotamia both suffered calamitous declines around this time and took centuries to recover. The Egyptian record-keeping systems appear to have declined into chaos and tales of the *Curse of Naran-Sin*, when 'flaming pot-shards fell from the sky' appear in mythology of the period. Egypt fell into anarchy and its productive agriculture ceased as the sun became hidden behind a veil of dust.

Yale University archaeologists digging a site some years ago in present-day Iraq discovered clay tablets describing major climate change 4,000 years ago, when arid conditions dried out the fertile lands and howling winds carried away the topsoil. A more recent satellite survey of the dried up lake of Umm-al-Binni, also in Iraq, showed what may be the impact crater of a giant asteroid, the explosive content of which would exceed a thousand Hiroshima-size nuclear bombs. James Ussher (1581-1656),

A November evening, on the ancient chariot road to Clonmacnoise

The Comet Donati as drawn in 1858. It is due to return in the year 3811

81

Protestant archbishop of Dublin, calculated the Biblical flood to have happened in 2349 BC. It is apparent that the Bible may hold the key to momentous past events related to climate change caused by meteor impact or volcanic eruptions. It is no coincidence that the possible impact crater in Iraq is in the same area where Biblical writers mention the great flood.

Theories suggest that the present day Hale-Bopp may have been much, much larger than the comet of 1997. It is possible that several parts of it may have become detached and struck the earth. Its effect would have been the same as an enormous volcanic eruption, changing the atmospheric conditions and blocking sunlight for a generation. The catastrophic effect on agricultural societies could have altered the belief systems of those societies, based as they were on 'Mother Earth' and her produce. For these agricultural societies, the apocalyptic sight of flaming debris raining down could have overthrown entire dynasties, especially those whose leaders

The comet
Hale-Bopp
photgraphed in
1997

claimed divine descent. If you come from the sky, and the sky falls, then whoever or whatever is 'out there' is displeased. Comet collision became a catalyst for violent change on earth. Climate change could bring a new god on the scene.

In summary therefore, around 4,000 years ago, people seem to have abandoned the darkness of the great tombs and moved outdoors to worship the sun. They stopped revering the dead to the same degree and began to create outdoor timber monuments and standing stones suitable for communal use.

Evidence from bogs and pollen taken from deep lake sediment shows a major decline in forest cover, beginning at this time as more crops are planted and society moved into farming on a much greater scale. A new god was there, perhaps replacing the moon, with day instead of night as a time of religious ritual. Major change had taken place.

An autumnal mist at Rathangan, Co.Kildare, a fortress of the O'Connor-Faly family

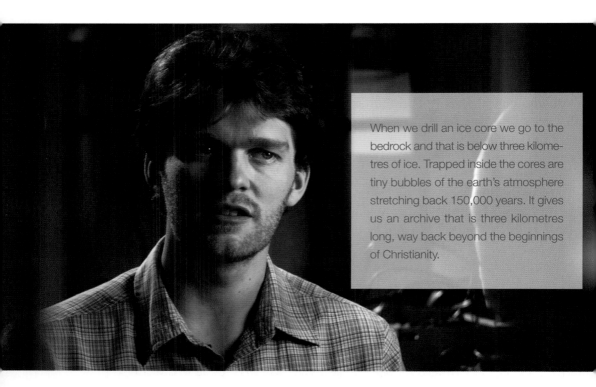

When we drill an ice core we go to the bedrock and that is below three kilometres of ice. Trapped inside the cores are tiny bubbles of the earth's atmosphere stretching back 150,000 years. It gives us an archive that is three kilometres long, way back beyond the beginnings of Christianity.

It's an atmospheric fingerprint, containing surprises... sulphuric acid and silicate ash, in the atmosphere for a period of nine years in the mid-6th century, a period described as famine with a dimmed sun. This has all the fingerprints of a volcanic eruption...

Dr. Bo Vinther, *Niels Bohr Institute, Copenhagen*

CLIMATE AND CHRISTIANITY

In the year 540 AD, Mount Hekla, an Icelandic volcano, erupted and may have affected Ireland in a profound way. Firstly the weather changed and summers became noticeably cooler, but this was only secondary. In the life of St Columba, Adomnán writes of the 'sky turning black and a red rain falling'. The volcanic eruption is confirmed in two ways. Firstly the tree-ring data shows a series of years where there is no growth recorded,

Ice-core research
station, Northern
Greenland

because sunlight was prevented from reaching the ground and also within Greenland ice caps, where volcanic dust has shown up trapped in tiny air-bubbles within the glaciers.

The climatic decline of the sixth century may have helped Christianity to become stronger, and perhaps the missionaries used the decline to show that their new god was defeating the old pagan deities.

In more recent periods, climate change has occurred several times. In the 14th century, the temperature dropped by several degrees centigrade and reduced the growing season. This cooling was followed by famine and the Black Death, a plague that killed one-third of Europe's population. Thousands died in Ireland's towns and cities during that period. There was another climatic dip four hundred years ago, when a mini-ice age struck Europe. Dutch paintings of the 17th century show frozen rivers and lakes, and across the continent famine and poor crops led to dreadful hardship for thousands of people.

In discussions about climate change, scientists in the 1970s believed that alterations of 2-3 degrees in the earth's surface temperature, especially in the northern hemisphere, took tens of thousands of years and that small local differences apparently happened within decades. By the 1980s, such changes were believed possible within thousands of years and, by the 1990s, such climate change was seen as being possible within hundreds of years. Now, it seems, climate change could occur within a decade or less and might last for a century or more.

But what if climate change had another dramatic effect, bringing change not only to the physical world, but also to how people think about themselves and society? This is what scientists believe happened at least twice in the millennium that ended just over one thousand years ago. Climate change brought major shifts in belief and understanding, the rejection of old gods and the beginnings of new religions. Without climate change, arguably, human society would be quite different to what it is today.

Tree rings reflect the difference in climate. The thinner the ring, the less sun, the less growth

Rathcruachain, County Roscommn, a vast prehistorc site with earthworks, tombs and standing stones and the birthplace of the Tain Bo Cuailigne

LiDar reveals the subtle surface contours of Tara

The British Israelites believed Ollamh Fodhla, an early Irish High-King was the Biblical prophet Jeremiah who hid the Ark according to tradition around the year 600 BC. They dug Tara in vain

THE HILL OF TARA

THE HILL OF TARA has held a place in the Irish imagination for thousands of years and is probably the best known and most famous of all royal sites. It was where priest-kings conducted elaborate ceremonies before the coming of Christianity, and the hill has continued to be important to Irish identity and contemporary pagan belief. The Irish word Temair, later anglicised to Tara, may be connected to the Greek word *temenos* and the Latin word *templum*, meaning sanctuary or high place.

Tara's summit, although somewhat flat to the viewer, has a complex array of monuments, the oldest of which is a burial mound, the most visible monument of this enigmatic site. It was the focus of ritual activity 5,000 years ago when Bronze Age royalty gathered for the burial of someone they respected. The Mound of the Hostages (*Dumha na nGiall*) became the tomb of a young prince or princess who was buried with a necklace of jet, amber, bronze and faïence, a tin-glazed earthenware. The beads are assumed to be from Britain but is has been suggested that they might have come from Egypt, suggesting the owners were of very high status. The burial mound is aligned between a sacred well, 'The Well of the White Cow', a venerated site and a nearby short stretch of parallel earthworks, which were probably a sacred avenue to the summit and the tomb.

An upright stone, the *Lia Fáil* or Stone of Destiny, was the focus of early kingship and ritual; legends say contenders for the throne had to circle their chariots at speed around the stone until their hubs screeched against its granite base.

Opposite page:
The church [now the Heritage Centre] on the Hill of Tara may hide the ceremonial entrance to the buried ritual enclosure under the hill

◄

Other standing stones can be found in the churchyard. One may have a sheila-na-gig (a carved female exhibitionist) on one side, but the figure is worn and has also been interpreted as Cernunnos, a god of the Celts.

But Tara was also a royal demesne for those living in the Gabhra Valley. The hill was not a stand-alone monument. It was the ritual and spiritual centre for a complex society, details of which have come down to us in the manuscripts. Their kings were both rulers and sacred personages and their inaugurations were moments of immense solemnity and tradition. Every king had a close kinship group of nobility, some of whom would hand him the special sword he would wield as ruler; another would hand the king the robes to wear. The participants were from hereditary castes, such as the O'Hagans of Tullyhogue who inaugurated the O'Neill with a wand of hazel, symbolising his kingship and his realm.

A bearded figure, perhaps an Irish king decoraes Kilteel chancel arch in Co. Kildare

Kings of Tara were the focus of magical powers and there were taboo's (*geasa*) that must not be broken. Most of these related to the presence or absence at boundary points of the *Tuath* (tribal kingdom) at specific times of the year. But Ireland's rulers also took advice. An Irish manuscript written in the seventh century is similar to the 'Mirror of Princes' seven hundred years later. It describes how the use of truth in judgement and the king as truth in person would guarantee a warm summer, a bountiful harvest and a safe society. Should his judgement fail, so would the tribe and the *Tuath*. Francis John Byrne, in his book on Irish kings and high-kings, suggests that these

Following page: The Hill of Tara, symbolic and ceremonal heart of Ireland for more than 5,000 years

A Cuneiform panel depicting what may have been the Indo-European precedent for laws related to the correct behaviour of kings

beliefs go back to Sanskrit literature and the Persian empire, where a massive stone mural describes how a king must not tell lies, and should he retain his integrity, so shall he keep his kingdom.

TARA'S MONUMENTS

On the Hill of Tara, the remains of twenty-five monuments are partially visible, but not all of them can be seen unless the lighting is very oblique. The site is best visited in the early morning or late evening, when slanting light throws into relief the mounds, earthworks and outlines of what existed millennia ago.

The monuments owe their poetic names to 19th-century scholars and antiquarians who tried to identify them with places mentioned in medieval Irish manuscripts. The 5,000-year-old passage tomb at Tara, for example, became known as *Dumha na nGiall*, the Mound of the Hostages, because it was the place where the symbolic exchange of hostages took place during the Middle Ages.

The Hill of Tara has a history as a place of ceremony and ritual stretching back over 6,000 years. During this long period it served as a highly ritualised cemetery, a pagan sanctuary and temple and also a place of royal ceremonial activity. Tara's monuments date from all periods, from the Stone Age to the medieval period, showing the enduring legacy of this ancient site.

Following page: Perhaps the eyes of an ancient god in the Mound of the Hostages, Tara

92

Tara, at the time of
George Petrie's
survey of 1837

Oıaßlaɔ

Aßlaɔ
Feaɲc Cheppán

Ouṁa an Cúɔuıḿ   Raċ Cholmáɲ Ṁc Chaelchoɲ

Caɲɲ Maċpaıõe Ua Neıll.

Oeɲȷol Ceaṁpaċ   Raċ aȷuɲ Scıaċ Chonchulaɲɲ

Caɲɲ Maċpaıõe Laıȷeɲ   Ceaċc Ṁael aȷuɲ Ṁöna

Cȷoɲ Feaɲȷuɲa
                Raċ Chonċoban Ṁc Neȷ
Seȷceaṁ na
Ceaṁpaċ   Ceaɲɲ aȷuɲ Meõ̇ɲ Chonchulaɲɲ

Claoċ-ċoßaɲ   Cȷeöuṁa Neȷ
Ṁuɲ na ḃ-cɲı ȷ-coȷuɲ

Claeɲɾeaɲca cuaɾ ɾ ceaɲcaċ
Raċ Ȝɲáɲɲe   Raċ Caelán

Foċaċ Raċa Ȝɲáɲɲe

Claeɲɾeaɲca beıɾceaɲcaċ   Slıȝe Ṁobluaȷɲa

Ceaċ Ṁıoõċuaɲca

Ouṁa na m-ban-aṁuɾ

Oopċa
Oluıɲcı   Slıȝe Cualann
Oall   öloɔ   Ṁael

Cȷoɾ Aõaɲnán
Raċ na Seanaõ   Ouṁa Aõaɲnán
                Cȷa na ḃ-Fıan
Ouṁa na õö   Cȷa Faıl   Ceaċ Maɲıɾeɲ   Caõaċ Choɲṁac
            Ouṁa na n-ȷıall
Cnoc õö   Raċ na Rıoȝ   Neaṁnaċ
                Foɲɲaõ
Cuċaɲ Choɲṁac   (no)   Ceaċc Ṁáne Ṁc Ṁuıṁeaṁaɲ
Laȷ   Ceaċ Choɲṁac
            Caċaɲ Cɲoɾɲɲ

Ceaċc Ceċen

Ceaċc Con

Raċ Laeȝaıɲe

            Ceaċc Maca Ṁoɲȷloṁaɲȷ
            Ionaõ aõnaċce Laeȝaıɲe

MONUMENTS OF TARA HILL RESTORED FROM ANCIENT DOCUMENTS.

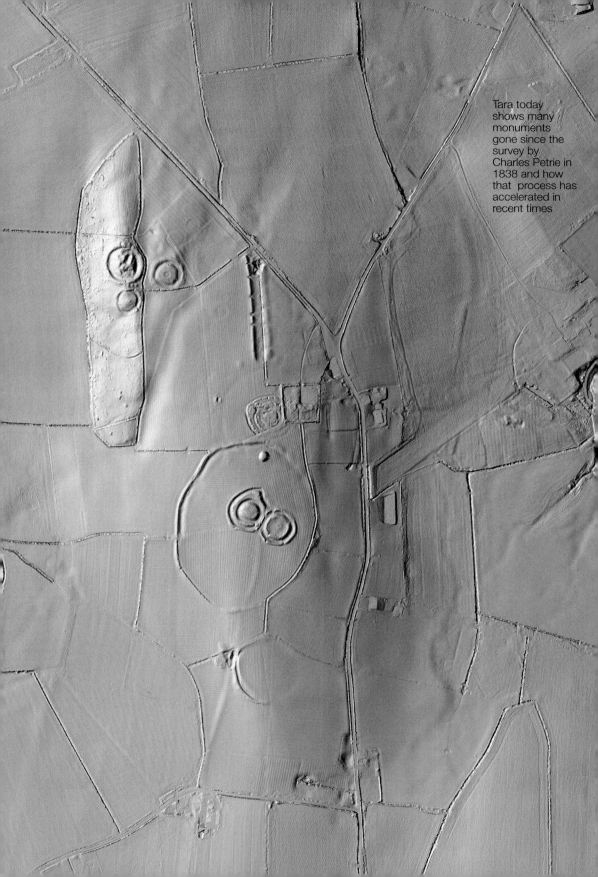

Tara today shows many monuments gone since the survey by Charles Petrie in 1838 and how that process has accelerated in recent times

STONE AGE AND BRONZE AGE MONUMENTS 4000 BC-600 BC

Mound of the Hostages (Dumha na nGiall)

This site may already have been in use before the construction of the passage tomb. This theory is based on the discovery of a stone flake from the Mesolithic period (7000BC – 4000BC) and early radiocarbon dates on charcoal finds beneath the mound, together with some early pottery shards.

More tangible activity started with the construction of the passage tomb, which dates from the 3rd millennium BC. Interestingly, there seems to have been a period without burial activity, which lasted for a few hundred years between the last Neolithic deposit in the tomb chamber (c. 2900 BC) until the early Bronze Age when burials were again inserted into the tomb and also into the covering mound. The passage itself is relatively small, just over four metres in length and one metre wide. It is fascinating that the remains of around 200 individuals (cremated and inhumed) have been found in the chamber and some 60 more in a stone-built cist near the entrance. The elite started to insert burials into the clay mound once the chamber was believed to be full. The societies of the Gabhra Valley used the Mound of the Hostages as a place of burial for more than 1,500 years.

The royal burial in the Mound of the Hostages

▼

The Mound of the Hostages was built around the same time as Newgrange and Knowth. This tomb is almost identical to the way these sites would have been when they started off. Also, the art here on the stone is the best evidence that we have that the Mound of the Hostages was created by the same people who built Newgrange and Knowth. An enormous number of human bones were found in this tomb during the excavation. In order to create space for the new burials, they had to dig down into the pre-existing remains of their ancestors. Between two of the orthostats was a cluster of skull bones, but there was no evidence for the bodies – as if this was not just a normal burial. To be buried at the Mound of the Hostages, you probably had to belong to the equivalent of the royal family.

Muiris Ó Suilleabháin, *Head of Archaeology School, UCD*

The last burial in the mound was a young lad of about 14 or 15 who was buried here just on the western side of the mound. He had a necklace around his neck made of many different materials. This might have been the equivalent of being buried with the crown jewels. The beads from his necklace seem to have come from Britain, which is unusual – whether the individual himself might have travelled is indeed an interesting question.   Muiris Ó Suilleabháin

A possible 'doorman'
outside the
Banqueting Hall of
Tara according to the
12th century Book of
Glendalough. Petrie
Survey, Royal Irish
Academy

There are also over twenty-five Bronze Age earthworks (very low circular mounds) on the hill. These may have been the burial sites of important people but they are not visible to the naked eye and were discovered only by aerial photography. Further testimonies to Tara's Bronze Age activity are two huge gold torcs, which were found on Tara in the early 19th century. They are now on display in the National Museum of Ireland along with many of the other artefacts unearthed during excavations.

> As a ceremonial space, Tara was a blending of natural topography and monuments, ancient and new, where the location and the architecture of the monuments were predicated by the desire to create a grand arena, one that lent itself to high ceremony and generated a symbolically meaningful place with its own distinct iconography. An encounter with this *temenos* in early medieval times followed established ceremonial pathways, prescribed by complex taboos that determined, *inter alia*, the pace and the sequence in which the landscape was disclosed. Approaching Tara was nothing short of a peregrination, mediated through an itinerary of traditional ceremonies and rituals at special, historical monuments and places, the lighting of fires and, no doubt, the recounting of epic tales.
>
> Conor Newman, The Discovery Programme, NUI, Galway

Northern-and Southern-Sloping Trenches (Clóenfherta)

These two ring barrows (circular burial mounds of earth surrounded by a ditch and an outer bank) are among the largest in Ireland. According to folklore, the gods destroyed both Clóenfherta as punishment for unjust judgement and malicious deeds.

The Fort of the Kings (Ráith na Ríg)

> At the core of the monuments on the Hill of Tara is the sanctuary of Ráith na Ríg. Through an inversion of the normal, its external bank and internal fosse may be an architectural motif intended to symbolise the paranormal, the reflexive, binary dynamic between gods and humans. This is the Otherworld into which the sacral king must pass, and it is the nexus from which he must eventually emerge as the conduit and intermediary between the human world and the world of the gods.
>
> Conor Newman

The Rath of the Synods (*Ráth na Senad*)
This quadrivallate monument (meaning four ditches) was badly disturbed when the British Israelites dug their way into it while looking for the Ark of the Covenant between 1899 and 1902. As a result of their destruction, being asked to do a field drawing of this site is a living nightmare for any student of archaeology. Romano-British pottery and glass, along with contemporary domestic refuse, were discovered when the site was scientifically excavated during the 1950s. With the help of these artefacts the site can be dated as functioning between the 1st and 4th century AD.

Lidar image of Tara showing [on left] the Sloping Trenches, [centre left] the 'Banqueting Hall' [centre] the Rath of the Synods, [right centre] Rath na Riogh

Banqueting Hall (*Tech Mídchúarta*)
This long sunken structure is the only monument on Tara from where the surrounding structures cannot be seen, thus creating the appropriate surrounding for a ceremonial procession to the sanctuary on the summit.

When one walks up this approach, the gaps in the walls hide and reveal structures that were probably the tombs of preceding monarchs, so the potential king walked through a sacred space as he approached the summit towards the Mound of the Hostages, the ultimate holy spot where the first or primary ancestors' bones lay.

Elaborate attempts to reconcile the gaps in the banks with the doors mentioned in literary accounts of Tech Midchúarta have perhaps preconditioned us to read the gaps as points of ingress, as doors. If we invert this notion, we can appreciate immediately that these gaps are, in fact, windows – windows that create, frame and therefore control what is seen and viewed. Because of its better condition, we can be far more certain of what specific views were offered through the gaps in the west bank, than those looking eastwards.

> As a semi-subterranean avenue, Tech Midchúarta may have been specifically designed to symbolise and to facilitate, in a tangible way, the journey or passage taken by the king into this nexus. It is a shared, or liminal, space, half in this world and half in the Otherworld of Tara, into which the king must immerse and surrender himself. The absence of fosses, which would otherwise account for the banks, evokes a sense that this is a spontaneous opening of the very body of Tara itself; it is of Tara. A critical moment in this genre of sacral inauguration is the hierogamy, the symbolic sexual union between, in this case, the king and the tribal goddess who is often portrayed or symbolised as the fecund land itself. Her acceptance of this earthly king, and her willingness to participate in union with him, are perhaps here symbolised by the opening that is Tech Midchúarta and the subsequent magical union of king and goddess. Conor Newman

Allowing for the fact that soil regeneration has raised the interior surface today, what the viewer sees through the gaps is the immediate foreground: that is the ground (literally the grass) alongside Tech Midchúarta. In fact, such is the height differentiation that the foreground becomes the horizon, and as such it obscures the usual panoramic vista across the Central Plain. And in this foreground are submerged tombs. Nearest, and visible through the third and fourth gaps on the right-hand side, are the almost ploughed-out graves of those who presumably ruled Tara. A little farther away, but appearing above the grassy foreground through the first and second gaps on the right, are the embankments of Ráith Ghráinne and the Cloenfherta (the Sloping Trenches), the three biggest ring-barrows on the Hill of Tara, all incorporating earlier tombs. The lie of the land is such that it falls away slightly more steeply to the east, with the result that through every gap along the east side, one's view is dominated by Skryne, offset against a background of the undulating plains of Brega. There are no tombs visible along this side of Tech Midchúarta, though future geophysical surveys may yet change that.

Cormac's House (Tech Chormaic)

This monument is a bivallate ringfort (meaning two ditches) dating to the 7th – 9th centuries AD. There are over 45,000 known ring-forts in Ireland. Ring-forts were not necessarily military fortifications, but more usually defended the homesteads of the better-off farming people in Ireland. A single bank encloses most ring-forts, but two or three ditches also occur, perhaps reflecting the status of their owners.

EXCAVATING TARA

Archaeological excavations at Tara began in the summer of 1952, directed by Seán P. Ó Ríordán, Professor of Celtic Archaeology at University College Dublin. His successor, Professor Ruaidhrí de Valera, completed the excavation of the Mound of the Hostages in 1959. During the excavation, hundreds of stone, bone, metal and pottery artefacts had to be analysed and classified; specialist studies of the cremated and inhumated human remains were commissioned, and scientific dates were established by carbon-dating organic samples.

Professor Muiris Ó Suilleabháin, Head of School of Archaeology at UCD, completed the task that had started decades before with his major publication simply but aptly called Dumha na nGiall – the Mound of the Hostages.

Twenty-five visible monuments are quite an impressive testimony to Tara's historical relevance but many more monuments have been discovered in recent years through non-intrusive geophysical surveys, aerial photography and LiDAR technology, showing the extent, complexity and importance of the site.

The defensive ditch for Rath na Riogh, a 300 meter in diameter Iron-Age hill fort is cut through the bedrock of the hill

An acronym for Light Detecting and Ranging, LiDAR uses a laser beam fired from a helicopter, to scan the ground surface and create a 3-dimensional map of unprecedented detail. LiDAR can peer beneath the vegetation, cutting through the leaves and trees, to paint a picture of the earth surface beneath. But LiDAR does have its limitations because it measures only the surface of the ground – and the nature of archaeology means that foundations and artefacts lie hidden beneath. A geophysical survey can solve that problem. The Discovery Programme and NUIG, conducted extensive geophysical surveys on Tara in recent years, revealing a wealth of new archaeological features and monuments.

Tara from the air is just spectacular. I think this is how the gods of Tara would have viewed their hill. In recent times a very extensive LiDAR survey was done over this landscape. This particular technology has enabled us to view the monuments on the hill in a way never before seen – it's effectively a facsimile; it's a carbon copy of the landscape as it is today. Ten or fifteen years ago we literally had to hack our way through the vegetation on the western flanks of the hill of Tara. Now, using the LiDAR system, you can do the same survey in a matter of hours. If you imagine that the LiDAR data consists of 137 million individual data points, then you can see that it might take several hundred years to conduct a survey in that sort of detail using conventional methods. It is a remarkable piece of work.

Joe Fenwick, *Department of Archaeology, NUI Galway*

During the course of a geophysical survey you are completely unaware of the nature of the features you are surveying. Only later on in the evening when you download your instrument onto computer and look at it on the screen can you see the subsurface features revealing themselves. Having employed our geophysical survey we can now more than double the number of monuments on the hill of Tara.

Joe Fenwick

During geophysical surveys a series of different instruments are used to measure the electrical and magnetic properties of the ground.

Archaeological geophysics has been defined as: 'The examination of the Earth's physical properties using non-invasive ground survey techniques to reveal buried archaeological features, sites and landscapes.' Simplifying a very complex technology, archaeological geophysics can be compared to taking a relatively expensive but highly cost effective x-ray through the soil.

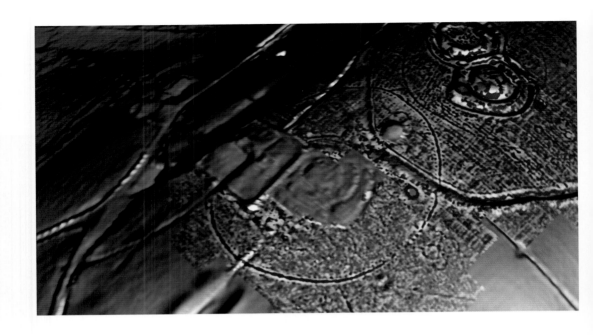

TARA'S HIDDEN SECRET:
FOOTPRINT OF A VAST ENCLOSURE

▲

The geophysical survey reveals the extent of the ditched-pit circle

A n ancient open-air temple, whose surrounding wooden posts would have cleared an entire oak forest, was discovered directly beneath the Hill of Tara. It probably dates from 2500 – 2300 BC (early Bronze Age) and measures about 170 metres at its widest point.

Joe Fenwick was part of the team that discovered the temple.

> The most exciting feature we found on the Hill of Tara is a vast oval enclosure on the northern side of the hill. It had remained hidden from view for thousands of years. This monument encompasses the Rath of the Synods at its centre, St Patrick's churchyard and the Mound of the Hostages. We know that this represents a ditch on either side of which were two massive concentric timber circles. For that reason we have called this monument, rather unimaginatively, the Ditched Pit Circle. To create a ditch six metres

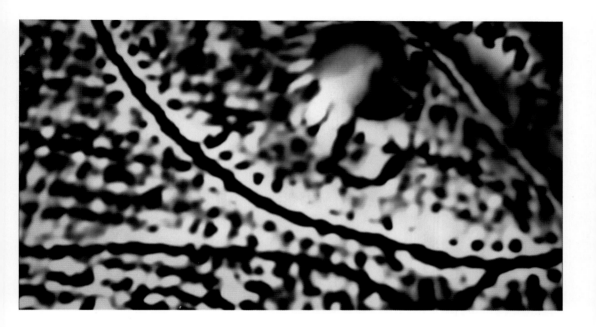

wide and three metres deep, which encircled the northern part of Tara's summit, would have been an enormous undertaking.

We also marked the position of one of the originally 150 or so massive timber uprights. They mark the outer perimeter of the ditch pit enclosure. It would have been towering several metres high into the sky and would have been set into large post pits. On the inside of the rock-cut ditch was another series of massive timber uprights. Our survey has revealed the footprint of this massive enclosure. We still do not know what the super-structure, the above ground view, of this monument looked like. If I were to take a guess, I would suspect that you had massive timber uprights onto which there were a series of lintels because it helps define the space, to define the perimeter. It works very well visually. The Hill of Tara had enormous ritual significance over the course of 5000 – 6000 years. It is therefore not surprising to find a monument on the scale of the ditch pit circle here. It has filled a gap in the sequence of monuments on the Hill of Tara. In scale the monument is comparable, for example, to the playing pitch and stadium of Croke Park!

Joe Fenwick

A close-up reveals the parallel series of post holes defining the inner and outer sanctuaries of the open-air temple

The extraordinary structure that once dominated the Hill of Tara, perhaps a temple or sacred space. Whatever it was, an entire forest would have been needed for the timber, which may have been richly carved with religious symbols.

MEDIEVAL FOLKLORE:
THE KINGS AND QUEENS OF TARA

The Hill of Tara, an important place since the earliest of times, has been the subject of myth, legend and history. It has been an important part of Ireland's cultural imagination since the time when writing first gathered the oral tales of pre-history. Tara enters history in a 7th-century list of kings called *Baile in Scail*, translated as 'The Phantom's Vision', wherein Conn Cetchathach (Conn of the Hundred Battles) receives from the god Lugh the names of his descendants who will rule Tara. The ramparts of Tara echo this theme of interaction between mortals and gods...they face inwards, to keep what was there inside the earthen walls. Part of the rituals of Tara involved the druids walking around the ramparts in a clockwise direction to keep the supernatural contained.

The kings of Tara were originally held to number 142, beginning with the *Fir Bolg*, a Celtic tribal group who may be an offshoot of the Belgae, a powerful grouping of peoples in Northern Gaul in the years around the Roman conquest.

In *The Kingship and Landscape of Tara*, scholars examined how Tara had become important to the dynasties that came to power in the centuries around the arrival of Christianity to Ireland. Those families commissioned elaborate genealogies, showing them descending from mythical kings who had lived centuries before, and having an inalienable right to rule Ireland, Tara had become the pre-eminent kingship by the 9th century. It is only then that the concept of High-Kingship became a realisable idea, and by that time Tara had been abandoned for centuries. The kings of Tara in the historical period were buried, according to tradition, in the mounds of Newgrange, Knowth and Dowth.

While some of the pre-historic kings may have been gods or mythical figures, some were genuinely historical and represent the struggles between the Uí Neill, ancestors of the O'Neills, the Connachta and the Ulaidh, whose historical base could have beeen either Tara or Eamhain Mhacha, the citadel they originally held near Armagh. The geographic kingship of Tara lay in the area of Brega, a territory that at certain times was a province as well as a kingdom. It was a point of conflict between many population groups which saw the possession of Tara as a way to the High-Kingship itself.

Opposite page:
A 14th century version of the *Lebor Gabhala*, or Book of Invasions details how the Firbolg were defeated by the Tuatha de Danann. These names may represent the Celtic tribes of the Belgae and Dumnonni

Library of the Royal Irish Academy

The 12th century doorcase of Killeshin church, Co. Laois may show its benefactor, king Dermot MacMurrough

Following page: A regal St Brigit decorates the stained glass in her cathedral in Kildare town. She wears a royal, Tara-style brooch and carries a manuscript whose leather cover has 8/9h century markings

Tara was not a kingship in the sense of a territory whose new king was elected on the demise of the incumbent; it was more an honour-title and perhaps a neutral ground between the other provinces. Francis John Byrne suggests that the provinces may have been not actual territories, but symbolic areas where various population groups gathered, their castes represented by different colours, similar to Hindu and early Germanic societies. Thus Connacht was 'white' and the land of druids and rulers; Ulster was 'red' and the land of warriors; Leinster was 'green' and the land of farmers, while Munster was 'black' and the land of the *Sudra* or subject tribes.

SOME QUEENS OF TARA

I n general, men are both the recorders and the recorded in history, more than women. The Hill of Tara, however, has many women recorded as queens, mainly as consorts to the kings, but at least they are named.

Caireann Chasdub

A dominant Irish warrior group, the Uí Neill seem to have created their wealth through raiding Roman Britain. Their ancestral 'mother' was Caireann, daughter of Scal Balb, king of the Saxons, according to the 11th-century *Leabhair Gabhala Erenn*. Her name may be a possible gaelicisation of the Latin *Carina*, and she was the mother of Niall (of the nine hostages). Although she is credited as Queen of Tara, she may have been a captured slave girl, 'promoted' in later literature to ennoble the Uí Neill's claim to the High-Kingship of medieval Ireland.

The Red Hand of the O'Neills, in St Columb's Cathedral, Derry, who claimed Tara ancestors and were generous patrons of Irish Church art

Angas, daughter of Ailill Tassach or Bressal Brecc

Angas is the first woman to be mentioned in the Christian records and the first to be converted from paganism to Christianity. She follows a traditional path of conversion in Europe, where the believing wife entreats and convinces an unbelieving husband to renounce the old gods. Contemporary tradition suggests that she is most likely a princess of the Eoganachta, the tribal groupings of Munster in the early Christian period who ultimately evolved into the MacCarthys, O'Donoghues and O'Sullivans and other prominent families of the southern half of Ireland.

Erc, daughter of Loarn

Erc's ancestry tale places her as a daughter of a Scottish king who marries a Gael of east Ulster and may relate to a dynastic alliance between the tribes of east Ulster and the tribes of eastern Scotland in the 6th century. The tribes of east Ulster, in particular, had many links with Dal Riata, or western Scotland, which was colonised by their ancestors centuries before. Inter-marriage with the Scots was frequent. The northern British king, Rhun ap Artgal, king of Strathclyde, was a descendant of Erc and later became king of Scotland in 897. This dynastic marriage may have reduced piracy and raiding along the western coast of Britannia and southern Scotland.

A 17th century tiara-clad Countess of Cork reclines in queenly state in St Patrick's Cathedral, Dublin

This charming painted wooden statue of St Catherine of Alexandria from the museum of Loughrea Cathedral may, like similar statues in Europe, have been the focus of intense religious devotion in medieval Ireland

Duisech, daughter of Tenga Umai

In a 12th-century manuscript that mentions her name, this queen of Tara is portrayed as an ousted wife, rejected when a king (see overleaf) finds a new consort. She became an example of the kind of practises that the reformers were against in Irish marital behaviour.

Sin, daughter of Sige, son of Dian
Sin may be another manifestation of the sovereignty goddess, this time in conflict with the new incoming Christian morality, which sought, initially at least, to restrict the number of marriage partners. She was the concubine who broke up the marriage of Muirchertach Mac Ercae, an early king of Tara.

THE END OF PAGANISM

The queens of Tara cover the period between pagan and Christian, and some at least were real flesh and blood people. We know that as Ireland became Christian, pagan beliefs slowly shrivelled, remaining however in the great narratives such as the Táin Bó Cuailigne. But what of the beliefs of the people who had but lately worshipped non-Christian deities? How can we understand the pre-Christian or magical thinking of our forebears? How do we access their states of mind or their religious thinking? Perhaps if we consider a particular faculty that everyone possesses when they are young, we might understand that ancient thought a little better. I refer to the open creative-mindedness of children and how they can be so absorbed in a game as to lose a sense of the here and now. There are few moments in adult life that have that enthralment, that captivation by something seemingly outside of the self. But the child's eye has a different take on life and, like the artist, it sees the world differently. To a child, the man in the party magician's costume is both a 'real' magician and someone in a mask; he is both illusionist and illusion. In early cultures of the past and in tribal societies today, the shaman is both someone they know and someone they fear, someone who can cure and someone who could kill. For the duration of the shaman magic, normal everyday logic is suspended. The imagination comes to the fore, 'make-believe' takes hold, and the mind experiences a form of mental alchemy.

The same phenomenon occurs at a controlled level when we sit in a cinema or become engrossed in a play. We enter into a different state of mind; we are in the cinema and in the drama, yet we know it is an illusion. When I sit in the theatre or the cinema, the lights go dim and I enter a dream world of a different time and space. A flat screen becomes a three-dimensional stage; people come and go, I travel to other worlds and feel emotions of fear, joy or excitement. It is an experience. In that 'space', somewhere between reality and a dream, things can happen. In tribal society, there was no illusion; the gap between the real and the imagined was closed and a creative fusion took place. It is the belief of many Catholics that when the priest says Hoc *est Corpus meum. Hic est enim Calix Sanguinis mei.* (For this is my body, this is the chalice of My Blood), then the wafer and wine changes from mundane yeast and grape into a corporeal entity, the saviour of the world. The sacrament is not understood as a symbol only, as in the Reformed churches, but as an actual miracle of the faith. Yet there is another part of this ritual. The onlooker must fully participate.

Deprivation from the world was also a way to godly knowledge and

salvation and for Irish holy men and women, it involved long periods of ascetic withdrawal, periods of fasting to achieve that divine union when all things become one.

The world today is not especially receptive to these moments and often decries belief and the enthralment it provides. On holy days in Mediterranean societies, however, there is abandonment to the moment as grown men weep when a wooden statue is carried from an olive grove to the village. In India, the mind-set necessary for such participation is called *Anya-Manas*, the Sanskrit term for absent-mindedness. It allows believers to enter into the world of the god and so lose themselves.

Strange conjoined cats, perhaps the symbols of concord decorate the base of Muirdeach's High Cross at Monasterboice in County Louth

An intense 17th century
St Patrick in the cathedral
of his name in Dublin

MEDIEVAL IRELAND
PAGAN TO CHRISTIAN

AS WE ENTER written history and the transformation of Ireland from a pagan to a Christian society, the first Irish-born Christians were probably the children of captured Britons, who, like Patrick, were brought to Ireland as slaves. These Christianised Britons laboured in the raths of the pagan Celts whose social structures echoed the descriptions of the Keltoi of Caesar's time, centuries before.

The transition from paganism was slow and partial at first and the old religion may have continued side-by-side with Christianity until the elite, their wives, druids and poets accepted it through conversion. Many of the saint's lives describe contests of magic and wizardry, usually with Christianity winning. Coincidental climate change may have been utilised in the persuasion process.

Britons were also trading with Ireland, and coins suggest they visited places like Dyfflin, the Norse city that became Dublin. The Brigantes of the North of England had a settlement on Lambay Island, off Dublin's north coast, and Loughshinny Harbour and its nearby promontory was a possible trading station, with Romano-British pottery discovered in the area. British Celtic tribes may have fled from the occupying Romans, bringing their legends and metalwork with them. The Celtic figure Setanta (Cu-Chulainn's boyhood name) is known as a warrior god of the Brigantes, and their goddess, Brigantia, probably became St Brigid, as the group were absorbed into Irish society and their origins lost. The first Christians thus established through slave and trading links with Roman Britain, settled in the east and south of the country, as evidenced by the papal-backed mission of Bishop Palladius to the 'Irish believing in Christ' in 431. Their early churches still remain in place-names such as Dunshaughlin, (Domnach Sechnaill, the church of Secundus) and Kilashee (Cell Ausaile, the church of Auxilius), both in Leinster.

Generally, it was long held that St Patrick was the first Christian in Ireland and the man who brought 'The Word' to Ireland. However, while he followed Palladius, tradition suggests Munster saints like Declan and Ailbhe were already prominent. Although Patrick confined his missionary activity to the northern half of the island, he was certainly the most successful missionary to come to Ireland.

Richard Warner of the Ulster Museum, has this to say on St. Patrick:

Everyone thinks Patrick brought Christianity to Ireland. Everyone is wrong! Christianity was already here when Patrick came to Ireland. He was a Christian missionary but he did not bring Christianity to Ireland. Most of the stories associated with Patrick – such as that he went to Tara and banished snakes – had nothing to do with what he wrote. Christianity was already here when he came. So he was a Christian missionary but he didn't bring Christianity to Ireland. Generally speaking, the Patrician period is opaque for archaeologists and historians. We simply cannot say as much about it as we would like. That is very, very frustrating.

Patrick was successful, and is remembered as the national saint. The church was the great civilising influence of early medieval Europe, and Patrick's mission in Ireland coincides with the beginnings of Christianity's European popularity. The Roman Empire under Constantine had been nominally Christian since 312, although large parts of Gaul and Britain remained pagan. There had been Christians in Britain since the year 207 and they had organised dioceses, when British bishops attended a 4th-century conference in Arles in Provence.

Further Roman and Romano-British material has been found in Counties Kilkenny, Limerick and Derry. The silver recovered and described as 'hacksilver', that is the crudely chopped division of pirates' loot, might also be the carefully weighed legitimate payment to Roman mercenaries, since one Irish king (Tuathal

At Cashel, a 16th century St Simon holds a medieval boat similar to those used by pilgrims travelling to Europe in the middle-ages

Teachtmar) might have used such men to recover his throne. Other Irish legends tell of an Irish prince leaving his home after a murder and joining the Roman army, to return many years later with spearmen (Galatae) and recover his kingdom based along the river Barrow. He gave them land as payment and their name in Irish, 'Laighen' or spear carrier, became the name of their lands: Leinster. In the early centuries AD, the rapid incursions of the 'Scotii', as the Irish were known, into Wales, Cornwall and southern Scotland prompted the British king Vortigen to seek the help of the Angles and Saxons to repel the invaders, thereby changing British society into 'Anglo'. The original Britons who fled the incoming Saxons went west and became the Welsh. Their descendants, who came to Ireland with the

Opposite page: The Ogham Stone from Kilmalkedar, County Kerry

Normans, took their toponym with them and gained the surname 'Walsh'.

Ireland's opaque history during the early Christian centuries may one day show further and more complex interactions between the two islands during the centuries of Roman Britain.

Ireland in the early medieval period probably had a population of considerably less than 500,000 and, after plagues in the 6th and 7th centuries, this may have decreased to 250,000 by the time the Vikings arrived. What is known is that around the time of Patrick's mission, agriculture began to improve, with a corresponding decrease in forest cover as more land was brought into production. By the 7th century, when records really begin, laws about land, trespass, fencing and the rights and obligations of landowners appear in the manuscripts. It is from this period that the majority of the 45,000 identified ring-forts emerge as primarily the homesteads of farming groups, with associated craft-working, primarily related to the functional ironwork necessary for agriculture.

The ownership of land for cattle or cultivation was in the hands of a Gaelic ruling class whose tenants lived as tenants-at-will, with little or no legal rights to their holdings. They were bound through obligations to that ruling elite and some at least preferred the later feudal arrangements within the anglicised lordships that abutted the Gaelic territories. The unit of measurement of agricultural land was the 'ploughland' of 120 acres, excluding *rivers, water meadows, moors, hylls and wodds*. This allowed for around 300 cows per eight ploughlands or around 1,000 acres. In England, the foot was standardised as a measurement in the reign of Henry I (1100-1135), and by 1272, the standard acre was reckoned to be 66 by 660 feet. The extent of arable land was measured by the number of days it took to plough it.

Very little evidence has been found to show what houses were like at this time. We know that many people lived in the beehives of skins or turves, but what of the upper classes, the landowning chieftains, poets and the more privileged people?

The manuscripts describe the chieftains living in timber halls, probably similar to the early wooden churches, but longer and wider. Some may have been quite large, with sleeping compartments along the side walls and a large hearth in the centre which vented smoke through a gap in the roof shingles. Smaller, wattle and daub versions of these hall-houses were found in the Viking excavation of Dublin during the 1970s.

In the chieftain's timber hall, the warriors each had a private compartment, called an *Imdae*, which faced into the main area where the feasting took place. The tales recount that a balcony above this area, a *Grianain*, was a place where the ladies could relax and look out across the countryside. It is probable that these houses formed the majority of dwellings for the

Opposite page:
Hebrew children
in the fiery
furnace are
watched over by
a curious for-
winged angel on
the High-Cross of
Moone, Co.
Kildare

The surrounding ditch of Rathurles, an early fortress of the O'Kennedy family of Tipperary, where fairs and markets were held until the 12th century

Gaelic aristocracy, and the manuscripts suggest that the interior walls were hung with alder-wood shields, together with furs and weapons, while the ground was covered with animal skins and straw. The timber walls may have been carved and painted.

Outside the hall were the associated buildings of the servants and men-at-arms, all surrounded by a high rampart with a wall-walk and stockade. A gate led from this enclosure into a cleared space used for addressing or inspecting warriors before battle.

EARLY CHRISTIAN IRELAND

The early Irish church took its inspiration from the training its monks received from St Ninian at Whithorn in modern Scotland and the monastery of St David at Glyn Rhosyn in Wales. The ability of the Irish monks to master Latin composition and Biblical exegesis was exceptional and, by the 8th century, the Irish church was respected, powerful and wealthy.

Ireland's first 'native' Christians were probably young noblemen like Declan of Ardmore, who may have returned from training in Wales to teach in Ireland in the early 5th century, some years before St Patrick. He was of a Waterford tribal group called the Deisi, who settled in south Wales and planted Ogham stones to mark their territorial boundaries. An Ogham stone of that early period found at Ardmore is reputed to belong to one of Declan's followers.

King David the harper on arm of the 10th century High Cross of Durrow

125

The cross at Caherlehillen,
one of the earliest Christian
sites discovered in Ireland.

CAHERLEHILLAN

In the early centuries AD, Armenia was the first country to adopt Christianity and the Roman Empire itself followed in 337, when the Emperor Constantine decreed that Rome would become Christian. As an alternative to paganism, it was attractive. Its dogma was easier to understand, it had an ethical and social message that was progressive and it was well organised.

In a hidden glen in County Kerry is the remains of an early monastic settlement called Caherlehillan. It may be the earliest Christian settlement so far discovered in Ireland. It was used for hundreds of years as a *cilleen*, a place where babies who had died before baptism were buried. The Church decided that since they had died without the sacrament of baptism, they could not hope to gain entry to heaven, nor could they be buried in holy ground. Distraught and devout parents came to this forgotten place to quietly bury their dead children in a place that had been sanctified by monks a thousand years before.

The Peacock stone at Cahelehillen

I like to think that Caherlehillan is the earliest dateable Christian site discovered in Ireland yet. We found a lot of pottery at the site and even though it may not look interesting at all, it turns out to be extraordinarily exciting pottery. It is very old and called B-ware. It comes from Antioch in modern-day Turkey. We have a very good date for it because B-ware pottery is precisely dateable to the late 5th century AD.

John Sheehan, *Archaeologist, University College Cork*

Post holes, those dark circular narrow pits that betray lost buildings, were discovered at Caherlehillan. It meant they had built a timber church, perhaps the first in Ireland, with crossed beams above the high pointed gable. These oak churches would have been quite small, holding a monk and perhaps a dozen people at most.

The church at Caherlehillan was only a very small building. One would not get any sense of how important it was just from looking at the reconstructed 3-D image. It does not look like much but we are actually talking about the earliest recorded church in Ireland. The four posts of the rectangular structure can still be seen today. One can only imagine how exotic the church would have looked to the people living around here who would have been used to circular pagan structures. Any pagan ritual complex in the late Iron Age in Ireland was circular in form. Here at Caherlehillan, in this little valley, people were making a point, clearly stating that they are a Christian community.

Tomas Ó'Carrigain,
Archaeologist, University College Cork.

Following page:
The interior of the early Christian church

The monastic site at Caherlehillen during the late 5th century

➤

Originally, the site was contained within a circular wall, probably of earth and perhaps two metres high. Within that boundary was the sacred space of the monks. They may even have come from the Middle East, since they brought a particular type of art with them, not seen before in Ireland. When somebody of great importance died in Caherlehillan, they decided to erect a grave-marker with a cross and something never seen before in Ireland: a peacock. The artists of Ireland had seen many types of art form – Roman, Romano-British, Gaulish, German and so on – but the art of the East was

probably new. The bird as harbinger was known in old Irish sagas as the carrier of many things: sometimes plague, sometimes news, often evil. Yet here was a special bird, a magic bird.

One of the cross slabs at Caherlehillan depicts a peacock, a bird which was not seen in Ireland until the 18th century. Originally, the peacock was a pagan symbol in the North African region. It was deemed to be a pagan symbol because its flesh was thought never to decay. St. Augustine took that famous motif and he basically repeated the pagan mantra: the flesh of the peacock never decayed and therefore it is immortal ... like the Christian soul. This is how the peacock entered Christian iconography.

John Sheehan

The peacock first appears as a religious symbol in those Hindu writings called the *Ramayana*. In this epic, the god of thunder, rain and war, Indira, became a peacock in order to escape the demon Ravana. The gods endowed the bird with the ability to kill snakes and to cry when rain was approaching. The blood and bile of the peacock was also believed to be an antidote against poison and, in India, those bitten by snakes inhaled smoke from its burning feathers. The feathers, in particular, were believed to ward off charms and spells and were used as part of the decoration of royal thrones across Asia and the Middle East. The pope still has a peacock feather held over his throne.

The idea of a peacock as a bird possessing non-decaying flesh may be a Christian-derived pagan idea, but the artistic origins may lie in Egyptian papyri, Persian mosaics or even the richly embroidered shrouds used for Christian burial in North Africa. For so many of the early centuries, Christianity was an Middle-Eastern religion and some of its exotica carried into Roman and western Christianity. Catholicism adapted candles, chanting, robes and incense; Isis and Horus became the Virgin and the infant Jesus and many other cultic ideas, such as eating the flesh of the god, became part of early Christianity.

SKELLIG MICHAEL

Following page:
The Skelligs, one of the world's most spiritual places

This dramatic rock soars 700 feet above the heaving and grey Atlantic and has a collection of monastic cells and a small oratory. Originally a pagan site dedicated to Manannan Mac Lir, the god of the sea, it was 're-baptised' as Skellig Michael some time in the 7th century. Monks, led by a St Finian, came to this barren rock and built two small churches, a

130

number of circular beehive dwellings and an oratory. In boats made of hide they transported enough soil for their own graves and a small garden. There are six stone beehives and two oratories near the top of Skellig Michael and these remarkable structures have survived almost 1,500 years owing to their dry-stone walling, which flexes under movement, giving strength to the building.

Vikings raided the island in 824, when they kidnapped the abbot, Etgal, who is later recorded in the *Annals of Ulster* as having died soon after of hunger and thirst. Monks such as Blathmhac (died 892) and Aodh (died 1044) ate a spartan but nourishing diet of ducks, puffins, razorbills and guillemots and their eggs. When the weather was calm, they fished for pollock and sea-bass.

Grellan Rourke and the Office of Public Works have carefully researched and restored these unique dwellings and have managed to retain the magic of the place, while ensuring its survival.

They really brought the drystone construction to a sophisticated level. The dry stone technique allows for a huge amount of adjustment in a building, so the stones are all maybe tightly put together but if the building is under pressure and moves, the stones tend to readjust, whereas in a mortar building it tends to act more like a monolith.

Grellan Rourke,
Architect, Office of Public Works

IRISH ART IN A CHRISTIAN CONTEXT

Ireland had an elite class of Christianised nobility willing to commission works of art, and the metalwork and manuscripts from Irish scriptoria in such communities as Clonmacnoise and Bangor were famous in these islands and Europe. The economic success and general prosperity of the monasteries formed the basis for proto-towns, and Clonmacnoise certainly seems to have developed streets, artisan workshops and many other aspects of urban living before the arrival of the Vikings, usually credited with establishing Ireland's towns. Christianity, as it developed, opened

A figure on Muirdeach's High Cross at Monasterboice shows Christ being mocked as 'king of the Jews', when Roman soldiers placed a purple robe around him and gave him a staff. He is shown wearing a Tara style brooch, to show his royal status

Ireland to outside influences in trade, art and the advantages of commercial society. Irish kings could see the usefulness of larger concentrations of people and the taxable wealth they could produce. Urban life was to their benefit.

It is when Irish art begins that we see representations of the people who lived at the time. What we see on the High Crosses are stone etchings, 'sketches' of the elite who upheld the laws, spoke the poetry and ruled the territories where Christianity took hold. Their faces probably acted as templates for some the figures on the crosses. Sometimes an art form can

The Skelligs continue to delight visitors and surprise archaeologists. One of the most exciting recent discoveries has been a previously unknown hand-cut stone staircase, almost invisible to the human eye which climbs the summit of the south peak almost 200 metres above the sea. To access the steps today requires climbing ropes and safety equipment. It leads to a monks private place of prayer, a hidden hideaway on the rock.

Stairway to Heaven.
Part of the 500 steps to the hermitage on
Skellig Michael

Careful conservation has preserved the cluster of bee-hives where the monks spent their lives of meditation and prayer in what must have been a physically and spiritually challenging environment.
Subtle restoration work has ensured that this rocky outpost of the spirit, retains its deep sense of aloneness and contemplation.

The Baptism of Christ with the two rivers Jor and Dan combining to form the Jordan. From the shaft of the broken cross at Kells

capture an aspect of an era. On Early Christian art we see musicians, animals, people, snakes, foliage and symbols of authority, both Christian and secular. Some of the clothes that enfold the figures may be the dress of the period. Perhaps the people carved on the High Crosses were alive at the time and posed as artist's models. The painters of Renaissance Italy included their wealthy patrons in allegorical canvases of biblical subjects, so perhaps an Irish king may be recognisable as a biblical figure on the cross he commissioned.

But the High Crosses in general are clear in their handling of both content and form, and in the flesh, as it were, are stunning, if weathering badly because of lichenous growth or atmospheric erosion. They span several centuries and in them we can see a progression of artistic development and taste. They would have been objects of immense prestige, and required a deep pocket and a discerning patron interested in sponsoring such extravagant pieces of art.

The Market Cross at Kells Co. Meath displays a riot of wild and domestic animals and warriors in combat, complete with swords and shields

◄

Left:
King David form the biblcal Old-Testament wrestles with the lion

Right:
The capstone on Muirdeach's cross at Monasterboice shows the steep roof and timber shingles of an early Irish church

◄

St Manachan's shrine shows the skill of Ireland's 12th century metal-workers

▸

19th watercolours by Alfred Du Noyer reveal the exquisite detail of Muirdeach's cross at Clonmacnoise

▾

Of craftswomen of the period we know little. One suspects they were kept out of the semi-mystical arts of metalwork and stone-carving. Manuscript illumination in Ireland was exclusively a male occupation. Elsewhere in Europe, nuns frequently were the calligraphers.

Laser scanning may reveal the identity of the stone-carver of the crosses of Monasterboice and Clonmacnoise, but whatever his origins, he was genius, a Michelangelo of the 10th century. There was nothing like his work in Europe at that time.

West face

East face

Cross of Clonmacnoise

EUROPEAN CHURCH DEVELOPMENTS

In the Middle Ages, the Christian church was organised into five Patriarchates – Rome, Constantinople, Antioch, Jerusalem and Alexandria – and, although Rome claimed a superiority, the others did not take it seriously. After the Arab conquests of Antioch, Jerusalem and Alexandria in 783, Rome's claim to pre-eminence became practical politics as Christendom shrank. The Arab advance meant the loss of North Africa, Syria and southern Spain to the Church and the forced independence of what became the Eastern Orthodox Church. The losses in the East were to a degree counterbalanced by the conversions in the West (Lombards, Visigoths, Picts) but Christianity was never to be a united Church again. The Popes, however, discovered the last will of the Roman Emperor Constantine and claimed that it bequeathed to them the right to temporal jurisdiction over all Christendom. In the anarchy and turmoil of early medieval Europe, the so-called 'will' was not enforceable but only so much forged paper.

In the Eastern Church, a doctrine of homage to the Virgin Mary developed through Cyril of Alexandria. It became formalised at the Council of Ephesus in 431, but it was another three hundred years before it began to flower, principally in Byzantium (today Istanbul) in the 8th century. Three theologians developed the doctrine: Andrew of Crete, John of Damascus and Germanus of Byzantium.

Left: Mor niBrien wears the headress of an Irish woman of high-status in the middle-ages.

Right: Modern plaster stature of Mary at a shrine in County Clare

The Greek Orthodox church was the source for the Marian hymn *Akathis-tos* and the prayer beginning Sub Tuum, '*We fly to thy patronage*'. The later cathedrals became centres of devotion to the Virgin Mary as magnificent structures such as Nôtre Dame du Chartres and Nôtre Dame du Paris were consecrated in her name.

IRISH CHURCH REFORM

H aving enjoyed a remarkable period of cultural and spiritual life, the early Irish church had probably passed its spiritual peak when the Vikings began their attacks in the 8th century. While undoubtedly still at-tracting those of a genuine vocation, it had, in a similar way to the church elsewhere, succumbed to the temptations of secularism. The Irish clergy were increasingly drawn from the noble Gaelic families and their benefices, or livings, were being passed on from father to son. This right of succession was recognised by a Brehon Law which stated: 'The tribe of the patron saint shall succeed to the church as long as there shall be a person fit to be an abbot of the said tribe of the patron saint, even though there should be but a psalm singer of them, it is he that will obtain the abbacy'. St Colmcille of Iona was succeeded by his first cousin, and the third, fourth, fifth, seventh to ninth and eleventh to thirteenth abbots were drawn from the same fam-ily.

The Irish church, however, provided a series of intellectuals who guided the re-emergence of Europe and the erudition in grammar and the classics they had acquired in the monastic schools showed them to be as good, if not better, than anything available to the continental courts they visited in the ninth century.

While clerical marriage was theoretically forbidden, it was quite common practice. The most striking feature of the Irish clergy in medieval Ireland was its hereditary nature and, as has been mentioned earlier, efforts to enforce celibacy came to nothing. Europe was similar, in that a distin-guished career in the church was a normal one for men of noble birth. For centuries, the diocese of Killala was the undisputed property and sinecure of the Ó Maoilfhaghmhair family, while even smaller parish churches were passing from monk to son.

Following page:
A medieval king, perhaps God the Father holds a sceptre of power

Clonmacnoise today represents a fraction of its original size and former importance. Lying beneath the present-day graveyard are the remains of streets, buildings and workshops. The riverbank was thronged with ship-builders and traders. The monastery was the educational, social and spiritual centre of this diverse and cosmopolitan settlement. But for a change in the circumstances of its royal O'Conor patrons, it might have become a major city.

The Cathedral at
Clonmacnoise,
begun by Abbot
Colman Mac Aillel
in the year 910

CLONMACNOISE

8

HIS GREAT MONASTERY, founded by St Ciaran in the 6th century, was endowed with land by the O'Conor kings of Connacht from its inception. Within two hundred years it had expanded to become a thriving town at the crossroads of the Eiscir Riada, the chariot road to the west, and the Shannon, the major navigable waterway of medieval Ireland.

Archaeologist Heather King has spent many years uncovering what lies beneath Clonmacnoise.

I think St Ciaran chose here deliberately, knowing this was a site that would be become popular. I think from the religious point of view he probably presumed he would get more souls to God, and the tradition to this day is very strong that if you get buried in Ciaran's soil you go straight to heaven.

Clonmacnoise doesn't fit into our conventional view of what a monastery would be like ... you've got ten churches extant and up to seventeen were there originally, because Clonmacnoise was not simply a monastery. There was a monastic element, but it was much more than that; it was a diverse community of monks, stone carvers, metalworkers and all the other trade and crafts that a medieval city would have had.

A lot of archaeologists wouldn't necessarily agree that Clonmacnoise was a city, but I argue that it was a city, in that it shows all the structural elements of a city in its organisation. It didn't develop any old way.

Importantly, they had developed a system of teaching and education, which was stunningly good, and this drew scholars from both Britain and Europe. Early Irish scholars were not the least bit bashful about their position in the world, because, having adopted the literature of Christianity and the Latin language, Irish schools were producing scholars every bit as good as elsewhere in Europe.

Heather King, Archaeologist, *Office of Public Works.*

Following page:
The 12th century
Lebor na Huidre,
compiled in the
scriptorium of
Clonmacnoise
principally by a
monk called Maol
Muire Mac
Celechain. It
contains a version
of the Tain Bo
Cuailigne, the
oldest piece of
literature in Europe
outside of the Latin
speaking world

*Library of the Royal
Irish Academy*

Clonmacnoise quickly became a thriving market centre as well as a monastery, and merchants from Gaul and the Mediterranean are recorded as visiting and trading with the Irish and the monks. Wine, salt and jewellery were popular items in Ireland, and Irish wool, beeswax and hides were commodities traded across Europe. St Ciaran's foundation grew into the greatest of all the Irish monasteries and fostered a school, teaching the works of Virgil, Horace and Ovid, as well as the scriptures.

There is certainly evidence that Clonmacnoise developed into a town and had many of the characteristics of a proto-city. Within the city were urban divisions known as precincts, with streets and buildings. Cobblestones, metal slag from art-foundries, post-holes from houses, slipways for a flotilla of ships and the foundations of an ancient oak timber bridge across the Shannon, 120 metres long and four metres wide have been found. This was no village. The bridge, similar to others in early medieval Europe, linked Clonmacnoise to the western side of the Shannon, where evidence suggests that further structures may have existed, including a Bruiden or hostelry. The monastic farmlands may have extended for 15 kilometres on either side of the Shannon.

It was a major centre for the production of manuscripts, the 11th-century *Annals of Tigernach* and the 12th-century *Lebor na hUidre* (Book of the Dun

Cow) were produced in its scriptorium. Later texts, translated into English from now lost originals, include the Annals of Clonmacnoise which contains a yearly 'diary' of the monastery. In addition to students from Britannia and Gaul, it attracted the greed of the Vikings and they plundered the monastery in 834, 835 and 842.

The church was robbed by a farm-worker about 100 years after its foundation and the Annals of the Four Masters recorded *'the theft of a silver model of Solomon's Temple, a silver cup, a silver drinking horn, a silver chalice, a paten, and other objects'*, presumably expensive gifts from the O'Conors whose kings were buried by tradition at the monastery.

There are stunning High Crosses and over 600 complete and fragmentary grave slabs showing the existence of important stone-carving workshops. Clonmacnoise was also a metalworking centre and produced the crozier of the abbots of the monastery. A possible fine piece from its workshops is St Manchan's shrine, which sits on an altar in a local church.

It was still a substantial settlement when the English attacked the town in 1179 as part of a campaign to subdue Connacht. They burnt 105 houses.

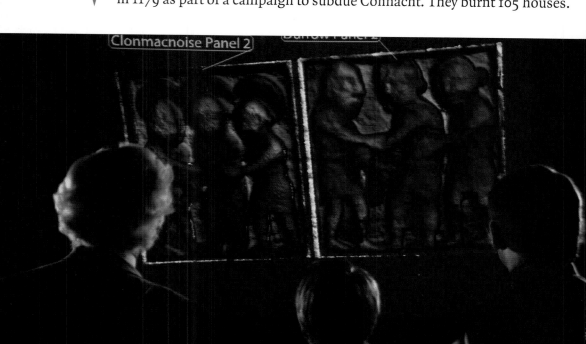

Clonmacnoise Panel 2

A watercolour detail from Clonmacnoise shows the hand of God releasing souls from the bondage of sin

Cross of Clonmacnoise.
Soffit of Circle.

Scale ½ full size.

THE HIGH CROSSES

I f there are particular works of art that typify Ireland in the eyes of both tourist and native, the High Cross is certainly near the top of the list. Ireland can rightly be proud of its Early Christian art and the carved stone crosses are its most public manifestation. The carvers worked in both limestone and granite, but found sandstone the most satisfying to carve, being easier to work with than the harder rock. The harder rock, however, proved the more durable, and clean lines and detail have survived, most noticeably on the 12th-century granite crosses of Kilfenora and Dysert O'Dea in County Clare. The sandstone details of many crosses have weathered badly.

THE CONTENT OF THE CROSS-PANELS

T he artistic inspiration for the form and content of the crosses shows Ireland's connection to the wider world of European religious art in the 6th, 7th and later centuries. The basic ringed cross, which is a feature of Irish crosses, can be seen on textiles of the Egyptian Coptic church and may have derived from such examples. Many experts further believe that wood may have preceded stone and the Ahenny, Co. Tipperary stone (High Cross) carving of a cleric in a funeral procession shows the monk carrying a wooden ringed-cross, perhaps the forerunner of the outline form of the stone. In addition to the ringed cross as forerunner, reliquaries (rectangular boxes of yew wood) with bronze filigree panels and edges bound in raised scrollwork were usually in a Celtic-inspired style. Celtic or Northern European inspired metalwork reappeared on the edge binding and interior panels of the early crosses, which were, in effect, stone versions of the wood and metal prototypes. The crosses at St Aethelstan's graveyard, Ahenny, show clearly how metal rivets evolved into stone bosses as the metal edge binding of a reliquary became the stone-carved corner of the cross.

On those early crosses, the panels along the front and sides showed no figures, but instead had intricate Celtic-type knot work and decorative animal relief, perhaps referring to the biblical Garden of Eden or a belief that Christ was also lord of the animals and of all vegetative life.

As the crosses developed, more influences came from abroad. Monks

A later, 17th century crucifixion from St Multose's church, Kinsale

had seen three-dimensional figure carving in Rome, both on the columns and the imperial tombs, and returning to Ireland through Germany or France might have seen biblical scenes carved on the panels of ivory which covered prayer books and missals. Painted frescoes from European churches were also to prove inspirational to the stone-carvers of Ireland.

These sources may have provided the inspiration for the three-dimensional biblical scenes carved on the crosses, which presumably helped to instruct early Christians. These *scriptural pictures* are like frames from a filmstrip of 1,200 years ago, yet no one is quite sure why some scenes occur more regularly than others, or why King David is such a popular figure. It may relate to the royal claims of the High Cross patrons, those kings of Connacht and the midlands whose monasteries the crosses enhanced.

In a time when the written word was rare, and understandable only to a tiny minority, a pictorial representation could speak volumes. They were first carved in the 9th century, when the *cross of the scriptures* was erected at Clonmacnoise on the orders of Flann, son of Maelseachnaill I, High King of Ireland (879-916). Based on scholarly research, it seems likely that the man who carved this particular cross was responsible for several more, including that of Durrow. The crosses are truly masterpieces, both informative and inspirational, carved with a hand that understood both the content and the nature of the material. The identity of the sculptor remains a mystery.

The twelve apostles from the High-Cross at Moone, Co Kildare

Today, information comes us somewhat relentlessly from a variety of media, but at the time of the crosses, most information and indeed entertainment was oral. What was on vellum, the scraped calfskin of the monasteries, was restricted to the eyes of an elite. The sacred books were probably revealed once a year on the relevant saint's feast day and no more. In the belief system of that time, the Bible contained everything about the world, from its origins in the Book of Genesis to its ultimate destruction in the Book of Revelations.

Peter Harbison, an authority on Irish High Crosses, comments:

The Irish high crosses are Ireland's greatest contribution to the sculpture of Europe and I think they're also a wonderful testimony to the spirituality of early Christian Ireland.

When the Irish were looking for a nationalist symbol in the middle of the nineteenth century, it is not surprising that they chose the High Cross as one of the most important, for, like the Tara brooch or the Ardagh chalice, it embodied the greatness of the country's Golden Age of artistic

The 11th century Round Tower of Kilmacduagh, County Galway, is almost 30 metres high

achievement in the early Christian period. Indeed, one could go further and say that these High Crosses are a very important contribution to European sculpture of the first millennium. For they are unique in having the surfaces of the cross decorated with many scriptural carvings illustrating the Old and New Testaments. As in the church frescoes of early medieval Rome, their purpose was to induce piety in the prayerful and, by means of 'clips' from the scriptures, tell a largely unlettered audience about the messages from the Old Testament, including those looking forward to the Gospels of Hope in the New.

King David, for instance, appears many times, doubtless because it was to his house that Christ belonged. But in being presented as symptomatic of the victory of good over evil, he may have been intended to be seen in conjunction with the important local kings, who, as we now know, were involved in commissioning some of the crosses, and who had their names inscribed on the cross-shafts so that posterity would not forget them. To those kings, and particularly the rulers of the Clann Cholmain branch of the Uí Neill, we should indeed be thankful for having been responsible for the creation of these splendid monuments which have stood sentinel over our old monastic sites for a thousand years and more.

Peter Harbison, *Archaeologist, Royal Irish Academy*

VIKINGS

The Vikings came to Ireland because it was a rich country, but poorly defended. It took Irish kings a century to impose their rule on the Northmen, by which time they had established their own towns on the coasts, the better to trade Ireland's goods with the rest of the world.

ROUND TOWERS, 10TH–12TH CENTURIES

There were at one time over 75 Round Towers, of which around a dozen survive intact. Many 'stumps' can be see on monastic sites, and several still show the effect of burning on their stone, perhaps relating to attack from the Northmen or Irish predators. Some towers rise to over 30 metres in height and the doors in the majority are around 3 metres from the ground. Their function was probably as bell-towers, although they were used also as places of refuge and storage for valuables. Their origins may lie in the bell-towers of monasteries such as St Gall, where Irish monks could have seen such structures and brought the ideas back to Ireland. The towers are sometimes found at monasteries where there was no known relic of a founding saint, so that having a tower might have proved a compelling attraction to the devout and an impressive piece of architecture for the local noble who paid for the work.

▲

The Rock of
Cashel at dawn is
dominated by the
square tower of
Cormac's chapel

ROMANESQUE ARCHITECTURE

This new style developed in Europe between the fall of the Roman Empire and the beginnings of Gothic architecture in the 12th century. It is a curious hybrid of French and English styles, with round arches and exuberant flourishes such as chevrons and heads, Cormac's Chapel on the Rock of Cashel being its finest example. It flourished at a time when the Irish church was reforming and shows the wide knowledge and cosmopolitan taste of Irish kings of the time. As a distinct style, it lasted for around 100 years and used an eclectic mixture of old northern European 'barbarian' art, with Celtic and northern European style vegetation, animals and human heads, often framed on the same door-case with Greek derived palmettes and a chevron frieze. The Romanesque church at Rahan in County Offaly has exotic decorations and architectural details similar to churches in Syria and North Africa during the 5th and 6th centuries and Armenia in later centuries.

The foliage, heads and profuse decoration, while seeming archaic, or nostalgic in architectural terms, even at that time, may have had more meaning to the people then than mere decoration. There seems little reason or precedent for such embellishment, yet something may lie behind the heads and chevrons that decorate the door-cases in particular. The confusion, as it were, of this 'Celtic' decoration on church buildings might be symbolic in its intent, rather than fanciful stone carving. Iconography may be the way to understand the profusion of design elements of both Irish Romanesque and indeed the metalwork of previous centuries. If we consider that the believers of pre-Christian Ireland saw nature as having a vibrant 'life', then taking inspiration or spirit from nature and placing it on an object carried over that life on to the object so carved or cast. It is perhaps not too much of a leap to see Christian art in the same context, as having a 'life', perhaps only symbolic, but nevertheless charged with a tangible spiritual presence which could protect or bring blessings to the wearer or to those who looked upon such objects. It is the source of the reliquary's power, the relic itself containing some of the high-powered holiness of the original saint. Many elaborate Celtic-style broaches produced in monastic

A delicate watercolour by Daniel Grose, shows the Rock of Cashel in the 18th century

Library of the Royal Irish Academy

workshops may have had this symbolic power and, as such, would have been highly valued. The tradition today of St Christopher badges or Padre Pio stickers is a continuation of that belief.

If, therefore, one considers that people in the centuries around the first millennium had a residual background belief in their pagan past, when decoration on objects had a magical or protective quality, then perhaps we may see the delicate interlace and entwined animals of Romanesque art as being that magic continued in a Christian architectural form. The door-cases, as mentioned earlier, may have been profusely decorated in order to prevent the devil from entering the church, to confuse him, knots especially being seen as difficult for him to undo and get past. Adding an animal to the knots made them particularly powerful. In particular, the snake is a prevalent animal in the interlace work of the Book of Kells, and in much Irish metalwork. Its strength as a motif suggests the recurrence of older celtic styles.

CORMAC'S CHAPEL

Built between 1127 and 1134, this beautiful church originally had frescoes covering the chancel above the altar, and may have used pigments such as lapis lazuli to colour the skies of Jerusalem depicted in its frescoes. Such frescoes, painted while the plaster was wet, were a feature of Byzantine churches, and derived from earlier, Roman models.

Excavations suggest that the chapel was built over an ancient graveyard and was orientated to face a grand *piazza*, with the High Cross as its focal point. The architectural inspiration probably derived from English and French Romanesque churches and has comparisons with the Benedictine abbey of Murbach, near Guebwiller in Alsace, (France). It has repeating arches in the form of a blind arcade along the west side of the building and paired, though slightly different, towers.

The north door is the royal entrance, its architecture enhanced by increasing the thickness of the walls to give the building a monumentality suitable for its royal users. The door-case has been compared to timber prototypes found in German timber houses in the Middle Ages. It was truly a royal chapel.

'With the passage of time the church became the state religion and acquired the patronage of local kings and chieftains ... powerful people ... and became less diciplined in the more stringent aspects of the Christian message. The term corruption may simply be the way local politics went.'

Dáibhí Ó Cróinín,
Historian, NUI Galway

REFORM AND THE END OF IRISH CHURCH INDEPENDENCE

Every organisation periodically needs reform and the early church was no exception. Reform in the years after the first millennium revolved around prising control of the monasteries from the descendants of the saints who had founded them.

A monastery in the early Christian centuries was the social centre of the tribal kingdom and provided the administrative back-room facilities that enabled the many *Tuath* (tribal territories) of Ireland to interact with each other, exchange goods and services and contract agreements. The monks and laypeople were educated and literate but, in many cases, not very religious. Ireland's monasteries were local affairs and the Church in Ireland was not a social force, nor the territorial power it was in Europe. But it grew and became prosperous. It owned vast tracts of land, which it both farmed and rented out to others, but it was still monastic in its structure. This meant

The Round tower of Inis Cealtra stands over the remains of a monastery founded in the 7th century by St Caimin. It retains an almost supernatural air of peace and tranquility

that the Irish church was not ruled in the European or English sense by bishops and archbishops but individually by the Irish abbots and abbesses.

In Europe, the 9th and 10th centuries provided an engaging spectacle of papal power politics, where different families fought for the right of appointment to the 'holy' see. In 882 Pope John VIII was assassinated, in 897 Pope Stephen VI was strangled, Benedict VI was smothered to death in 984, and John XII, appointed pope at the age of eighteen, died, apparently of 'amorous excess while making love'. Despite this, the Church was gaining in power, although there was a struggle between the Emperor Henry IV of Germany and

Pope Gregory I. The end of this struggle for power resulted in the papacy becoming a player in European politics, effectively combining church and state. This was in contrast to the Irish position, which kept the two separate. Notions that the Irish church was corrupt, or at least in need of European moral guidance, seem misguided when compared to the papal norm.

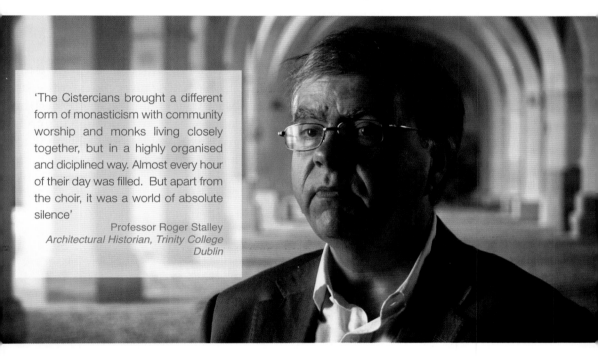

'The Cistercians brought a different form of monasticism with community worship and monks living closely together, but in a highly organised and diciplined way. Almost every hour of their day was filled. But apart from the choir, it was a world of absolute silence'

Professor Roger Stalley
Architectural Historian, Trinity College Dublin

Most of the early Irish churches were small stone buildings surrounded by the huts of their brethren and often by a greater settlement. They had originally been founded by saints and were now ruled by an hereditary elite class called *comarba* or descendants of the founder. This developed because the monastic lands were first granted by the local Gaelic lord, who frequently requested that a family member be ordained an abbot. This removed a potential rival from the scene and set him up with the estate and prestige his lineage demanded. Naturally, the said abbot wanted his family to continue this arrangement, so marriage and concubinage developed, with some clerics having several children by both wife and mistress. Many of the *comarba* were not clerics and so the actual performance of religious functions became neglected. Because the Irish church was in need of reform, certain Irish Christians began to look outside.

The reform, however, began internally. Since the 8th century, the Vikings had intermarried with the Irish and, notwithstanding the fantasy that the Vikings had fled the country after the Battle of Clontarf, many of the towns they had founded had grown to become Christian-Hiberno-Norse cities. They were devout but independent.

For the Hiberno-Norse Christians of Dublin, Limerick and Waterford, having their urban churches ruled by people whose principal interest was to secure high farmland rentals and jobs for their families upset their urban minds. They began to look outside Ireland for help. With this aim in mind, the city urban-Irish in the 11th century began sending their bishops to Canterbury for consecration, seeing in the English diocesan organisation something that could work in Ireland. The English church therefore took an interest in Ireland.

A medieval mermaid holds her star-shaped mirror to warn of lust and vanity on the wall of Clontuskert church, County Galway

REFORM GATHERS PACE

In 1093 and 1103 St Anselm of Canterbury wrote to King Muirteach Uí Briain of Munster urging him to reform the abuses of the Church. But before England could become involved ecclesiastically, reforms were introduced into the Irish church and bishops Cellach of Armagh and Malchus of Lismore joined bishop Gilla Espuic of Limerick in promoting them countrywide. In 1111 Muirteach Uí Briain opened the reforming synod of Rath Breasil, near Cashel. The Irish church was reorganised on English lines, with dioceses, two archbishops and twenty-four bishops. It took, however, forty years for the reforms to be fully implemented, since the Irish monasteries were reluctant to change and so hindered the work. Cellach of Armagh ordained a young reformer called Malachy, who would become the engine of change. But Malachy was not content to allow church reform in Ireland to creep along and be derailed by internal politics and power alliances. For the changes needed to bring the Irish church up to international standards of the time, outside and expert help might be needed. Malachy found what he was look-

The clean lines of Cistercian architecture at Clairvaux, in eastern France

ing for in the order of Cistercian monks, founded by St Bernard.

Returning from his first visit to Rome, Malachy stayed at Clairvaux where he met St Bernard and admired the Cistercian way of life. This was the return to monasticism that he had sought, another form of ascetic life that would be spiritually apart from the world yet fully within it, ensuring that the monastic order was able to work and pray, teach and educate. He left companions behind to train and by 1141, they were ready to return.

A NEW STYLE OF CHURCH BUILDING ARRIVES IN IRELAND

Irish church architecture was, for the early Christian centuries, entirely in wood, following the native tradition. Of these buildings, nothing has remained, owing to the ephemeral nature of timber and intermittent fire damage caused both accidentally and by intent. Ireland had many forests of oak and that solid timber probably formed the structural posts of the early churches. Manuscripts mention the durable construction of such buildings and the craftsmanship of the carpenters. The wall-panels were mostly interwoven from willow and hazel, then covered with clay to form walls of wattle. The roof would have been either thatch or shingles of yew wood, as mentioned in the Book of Moling, the 6th-century founder of the monastery known as St Mullins in County Carlow. Small timber churches were approximately 5 metres long by 2.5 metres wide, although several are recorded as being quite large; St Brigid's church in County Kildare may have been several times that size. The later beehive huts of such famous oratories as Skellig Michael were widely scattered across the Dingle Peninsula and reflected in stone the simple hide-covered dwellings of medieval farming people and their families.

MELLIFONT AND THE ARRIVAL OF GOTHIC

Fons Mellis The Fount of Honey

In general, Cistercian monasteries were built in remote places away from medieval towns or cities. The Cistercians were not power-brokers and

what focus they had outside of the liturgy seems to have been agricultural rather than political. The church they built followed a similar plan to the original at Clairvaux and Robert the Cistercian came from France to supervise its construction. The site was given by Donough O'Carroll, who supported Malachy of Armagh and his movement to bring the Irish church out of the orbit of Canterbury and nearer to Rome.

St Malachy
Courtesy, Musee des Beaux Arts, Dijon

The church was laid out as a cross, with a high vaulted nave where the side arms met the main body. To the south of the church were the domestic quarters of the monks, usually surrounding the cloister walk where daily prayer and contemplation took place. On the east of the cloisters was the chapterhouse where monks would gather to hear readings from the scriptures, the south contained the kitchen and refectory, the west held the stores, while above were the dormitories for the monks and lay brethren. All

A computer image of St Mary's abbey in Dublin, once the country's richest Cistercian monastery, but now buried beneath the cobbles of the markets behind Capel Street

in all, the monasteries of the continental orders, Cistercians, Augustinians and Franciscans were self-enclosed communities, ordered, planned and self-sufficient, and at Mellifont, despite its ruined appearance, we can glimpse the size and complexity of that time. The elegant lavabo, or wash-house, where the monks could clean themselves before and after eating is the only one to survive in Ireland.

The monastery began as an Irish and French foundation but, following the arrival of the Anglo-Normans, it came under the control of English monks, who tried to remove it from Irish domination. Over the following centuries, it accumulated a 48,000-acre estate, which brought a huge income to the monks and brothers. The abbot of Mellifont was entitled to a seat in the House of Lords at Westminster, and the monastery, similar to its brethren in Europe, moved from being a place of prayer and worship to being a seat of power and wealth. The Cistercians were good at business. Monks in general, however, were responsible for much improvement in Irish agriculture. The Augustinians in the Barrow valley in County Kilkenny introduced selective breeding in their sheep herds and developed a thriving international wool trade with what would be called 'export agents' in Waterford and Dublin.

Many Cistercian monasteries were destroyed during and following the Reformation of the 16th century and Mellifont did not escape. It was dismantled as a monastery and used as a house before its great high nave and tall gothic windows were broken down and the site almost levelled in the 17th century. What remains is a perverse monument to the violent struggles of that period.

THE END OF GAELIC AUTONOMY AND THE ARRIVAL OF THE ANGLO-NORMANS

I n the summer of 1166, Rory O'Conor, the new high king convened a great gathering of the Gaelic aristocracy at Tlaghta, near Athboy, Co. Meath. At this meeting, presided over by St Gaelasius, were O'Rourke, prince of Breffni, Dunchad, prince of Oriel, Eochaid, prince of Ulaidh, Ó'Melachlainn, prince of Tara Mac Torquil, jarl of Dublin and many others. They were meeting to divide Ireland between the royal families and restore the political structure of Ireland after an affray, which had led to the death of Muirchertach MacLochlainn, the high king.

Conspicuous by his absence was Dermot MacMurrough, king of Leinster, who had resumed an affair with O'Rourke's wife, Dervorgilla. O'Rourke decided to have revenge on MacMurrough by attacking his kingdom.

Dermot was not a popular overlord and finding friends to defend his Leinster lands against the cuckolded O'Rourke proved difficult. His kingdom seemed lost, but he was resourceful and devious and he fled to the court of England's Henry II, who owed him a favour, Dermot having lent Henry his Wexford fleet to defeat an uprising. Henry gave permission to recruit men from Bristol and south Wales and Dermot did so, promising land and rewards to those who would accompany him to Wexford and recover his kingdom.

Slightly over 400 Normans arrived on 1 May 1167, followed by followers and servants from Flanders and Brittany. They too in their own way became Irish and left a further enduring legacy in stone.

The figure of St Francis watches the empty cloisters of Askeaton friary, burnt and looted in September 1579 by the army of Nicholas Malby. The close of the 16th century saw the end of Gaelic Ireland and the destruction of the culture that had existed since the time of Tara and its kings

RECOMMENDED READING
GENERAL BOOKS ON IRISH HISTORY AND ARCHAEOLOGY

Aalen, F.H.A., K. Whelan, M. Stout, (eds.), *Atlas of the Irish Rural Landscape*, Cork University Press, 1997

Arnold, Bruce, *A Concise History of Irish Art*, Thames & Hudson, 1969

Barry, Terry, *A History of Settlement in Ireland*, Routledge, 2000

Darvill, Timothy, *The Concise Oxford Dictionary of Archaeology*, Oxford University Press, 2008

Dudley-Edwards, Ruth, *Atlas of Irish History*, Routledge, 1973

Duffy, Seán (ed.), *Atlas of Irish History*, Gill & Macmillan, 1997

Harbison, Peter, *Guide to National and Historic Monuments of Ireland*, Gill & Macmillan, 1992

——, *Treasures of the Boyne Valley*, Gill & Macmillan, 2003

Harbison, P., H. Potterton, and J. Sheehy, *Irish Art and Architecture: From Prehistory to the Present*, Thames & Hudson, 1978

Mitchell, F. and M. Ryan, *Reading the Irish Landscape*, Town House, 1998

Mulligan, Paul, *A Short Guide to Irish Antiquities*, Wordwell, 2005

Newman, C. and A. Halpin, *Ireland: An Oxford Archaeological Guide*, Oxford University Press, 2006

Ó Cróinín, Dáibhí (ed.), *Prehistoric and Early Ireland. A New History of Ireland*, vol. 1, Royal Irish Academy, 2005

Ó Ríordáin, Seán, P., *Antiquities of the Irish Countryside*, Methuen, 1966

Ryan, Michael (ed.), *Irish Archaeology Illustrated*, Country House, 1994

Wallace, P. F., and R. Ó Floinn, *Treasures of the National Museum of Ireland: Irish Antiquities*, Gill & Macmillan, 2002

EPISODE ONE: PRE-HISTORIC IRELAND

Baillie, Mike, *A Slice through Time – Dendrochronology and Precision Dating*, Routledge, 1995

——, *Exodus to Arthur – Catastrophic Encounters with Comets*, Batsford, 1999

Bergh, Stefan, *Landscape of the monuments. A study of the passage tombs in the*

Cúil Irra region, Co. Sligo, Ireland. Riksantikvarieämbetet Arkeologiska Undersökningar, 1995

Burenhult, Göran, *The Illustrated Guide to the Megalithic Cemetery of Carrowmore, Co. Sligo*, Göran Burenhult, 2001

Chadwick, Nora, *The Celts*, Pelican Books, 1979

Cooney, G. and E. Grogan, *Irish Pre-History*, Wordwell, 1994

Cunliffe, Barry, *The Celtic World*, Greenwich House, 1986

——, *Facing the Ocean*, Oxford, 2001

Edel, Doris, *The Celtic West and Europe*, Four Courts Press, 2001

Eogan, George, *Knowth and the Passage-tombs of Ireland*, Thames & Hudson, 1986

Fenwick, Joe (ed.), *Lost and Found: Discovering Ireland's Past*, Wordwell, 2003

Green, Miranda, *The Celtic World*, Routledge, 1995

——, *Gods of the Celts*, Barnes & Noble, 1986

Harbison, Peter, *Pre-Christian Ireland. From the First Settlers to the Early Celts*, Thames & Hudson, 2002

Herity, M. and G. Eogan, *Ireland in Prehistory*, Routledge, 1970

Jones, Carlton, *Temples of Stone. Exploring the Megalithic Tombs of Ireland*, The Collins Press, 2007

Lalor, Brian, *The Irish Round Tower*, The Collins Press, 1999

Mallory, J.P., *In Search of the Indo-Europeans*, Thames & Hudson, 1989

McCafferty, P. and M. Baillie, *The Celtic Gods: Comets in Irish Mythology*, Tempus, 2005

Newman, Conor, *Tara: An Archaeological Survey. Discovery Programme Monographs 2*, 1998

Ó hÓgain, Daithi, *The Sacred Isle – Belief and Religion in Pre-Christian Ireland*, The Collins Press, 1999

O' Kelly, Michael J., *Early Ireland – An Introduction to Irish Prehistory*, Cambridge University Press, 1995

Ó Suilleabháin, Muiris, *Duma na nGiall: The Mound of the Hostages, Tara*, Wordwell & UCD School of Archaeology, 2005

Raftery, Barry, *Pagan Celtic Ireland: The Enigma of the Irish Iron Age*, Thames & Hudson, 1997

Slavin, Michael, *The Book of Tara*, Wolfhound Press, 1996

Stout, G. and M. Stout, *Newgrange*, Cork University Press, 2008

Twohig, Elizabeth Shee, *Irish Megalithic Tombs*, Shire Archaeology, 2004

Waddell, J., *The Prehistoric Archaeology of Ireland*, Wordwell, 2000
Warner, Richard, *The Earliest History of Ireland*, in Ryan, Michael (ed.), *Irish Archaeology Illustrated*, Country House, 1994

EPISODE TWO: EARLY CHRISTIAN IRELAND

Byrne, Francis J., *Irish Kings and High Kings*, Four Courts Press, 1973
Carney, James, *Mediaeval Irish Lyrics*, Dolmen Press, 1967
de Paor, Liam, *Excavations at Mellifont Abbey, Co. Louth*, Proceedings of the Royal Irish Academy 68C (2), 1969
de Paor, L. and M. de Paor, *Early Christian Ireland*, Thames & Hudson, 1958
Dillon, Myles, *Early Irish Literature*, University of Chicago Press, 1948
Di Martino, Vittorio, *Roman Ireland*, The Collins Press, 2003
Duffy, Seán, *Ireland in the Middle Ages*, Gill & Macmillan, 1997
Edwards, Nancy, *The Archaeology of Early Medieval Ireland*, Routledge, 2000
Flower, Robin, *The Irish Tradition*, Lilliput Press, 1994
Freyne de, Seán, *The Great Silence*, Mercier Press, 1965
Greene, D. and F. O'Connor, *Irish Poetry: AD 600 – 1200*, Macmillan, 1967
Harbison, Peter, *Irish High Crosses*, The Boyne Valley Honey Company, 1994
——, *Pilgrimage in Ireland. The Monuments and the People*, Syracuse University Press, 1992
Henry, Françoise, *Irish High Crosses*, Three Candles Press Ltd., 1964
——, *Irish Art in the Early Christian Period*, Methuen & Co, 1940
Kelly, Fergus, *Early Irish Farming*, Dublin Institute for Advanced Studies, 2000
King, Heather A., *Clonmacnoise Studies*, 2 vols, Wordwell, 1998 – 2003
Kinsella, Thomas, *The Táin*, Oxford University Press, 1988 Revised edition
Laing, Lloyd, *Late Celtic Ireland and Britain*, Methuen, 1975
Leask, Harold, *Irish Churches and Monastic Buildings*, 3 vols, Dundalgan Press, 1955-60
Mac Niocaill, Gearoid, *Ireland before the Vikings*, Gill & Macmillan, 1972
Manning, Conleth, *Early Irish Monasteries*, Country House, 1995
Sheehan, John & Michael A. Monk, (eds.), *Early Medieval Munster – Archaeology, History and Society*, Cork University Press, 1998

Ó Corráin, Donncha, *Ireland before the Normans*, Gill & Macmillan, 1972

Ó Cróinín, Dáibhí, *Early Medieval Ireland: 400 - 1200*, Longman Group Ltd, 1995

Richardson, H. and J. Scarry, *Irish High Crosses*, Mercier Press, 1990

Rourke, Grellan (et al), *The Forgotten Hermitage of Skellig Michael*, University of California Press, 1990

Stalley, Roger, *Irish High Crosses*, Country House, 2004

——, *The Cistercian Monasteries of Ireland: An Account of the History, Art and Architecture of the White Monks in Ireland from 1142 to 1540*, Yale University Press, 1987

INDEX

A

A New Style of Church Building Arrives
    In Ireland, 164
Aethelstan, Saint, 150
Africa, North, 139
Ahenny, County Tipperary, 150
Ailbhe, Saint, 120
Áine, Great Earth Mother, 67
Alexandria, patriarchate, 139
Analysis of Cremated Remains at
    Knowth, 62–63
Andrew of Crete, theologian, 139
Angas, Queen of Tara, daughter of Ailill
    Tassach or Bressal Brecc, 112
Angles, people, 121
Annals of Clonmacnoise, 148
Annals of the Four Masters, 148
Annals of Tigernach, 146
Annals of Ulster, 131
Anselm, Saint, 163
Antioch, patriarchate, 139
Antrim, County, 25
Anu, see Áine
Aodh, Skellig Michael monk, 131
Archaeology, 8, 21–23
Ardee Bog, 25–26
Ardmore, County Waterford, 76, 125
Armagh, city, 109
Armagh, County, 20
Armenia, 127, 157
Astronomy and early Irish history, 20–
    21, 51
Augustine, Saint, 130
Augustinians, monastic monks, 166-7

B

Baillie, Mike, 77–80
Balkans, the, 25
Baltic, the, 36, 42
Bangor, 132
Barnenez, tombs in Brittany, 47
Barrow, the river, 121
Barrow Valley, Kilkenny, 167
Beara Peninsula, 35
Belgae, grouping of peoples in Northern
    Gaul, 109
Benedict VI, pope, 60
Benedictine Abbey, Murbach, 158
Bergh, Stefan, 46, 47, 48–49, 50
Bernard of Clairvaux, Saint, 164
Bible, 81–82
Black Death, plague, 85
Blathmhac, Skellig Michael monk, 131
Book of Ballymote, 34
Book of Genesis, 153
Book of Kells, 158
Book of Leinster, 98
Book of Moling, 164
Book of the Dun Cow,
    see Lebor na hUidre
Book of Revelations, 153
Boyne Valley
    people, 57
    tombs, 13, 30, 39, 43, 53, 55, 58
Brega, plains of, 101, 109
Brehon Law, 19, 140
Bricklieve Mountains, 51
Brigantes, pre Christian tribe, 119
Brigantia, Brigantes goddess, 119
Brigid, Saint, 111
    see also Brigantia

Bristol, 167
Britain
  tombs, 57, 89
  raids by the Irish, 112, 121–2
Britannia, 113, 148
Brittany, 167
  art from, 14, 65
  and Irish population, 28, 42
  tombs, 47, 67
Bronze Age
  climate change, 79
  metalwork, 36, 73
  pottery, 39
  and religion, 20
  tomb building, 13, 41, 89, 96, 98, 104
  trade, 35–37
Buckley, Laureen, 62–63
Byrne, Francis John, 90, 110
Byzantium, 139
  churches, 158

C
Caherlehillan, 127–30
Cailleach, hag or witch, 53–54
  see also Sliabh na Cailleach
Caireann Chasdub, Queen of Tara, 112
Calliaghstown, County Westmeath, 54
Canada and pre-historic landscape, 14
Canterbury, 162, 165
Carrowkeel Megalithic cemetery, 51–52
Carrowkeel Ware, see Pottery
Carrowmore tombs, 43, 44–50, 51
Catholic Church, the, 127
Ceide Fields, County Mayo, 30
Cell Ausaile, the church of Auxilius,
  see Kilashee
Cellach, of Armagh, bishop, 163
Celtic
  art, 57–58
  Ireland, 36
  tribes, 119
Cernunnos, Celtic god, 90
Cetchathach, Conn, see Conn of the
  Hundred Battles
Cha de Parada, tombs in Galicia, 47

China, 79
Christ, 130, 133, 155
Christian art, 157
Christianity, 127, 130, 139
  and climate change, 14
  in Ireland, 19. 109, 115–7, 119, 120,
    125, 132–3
Christopher, Saint, 158
Ciaran, Saint, 145, 146
Cistercians, monastic monks, 19, 164–7
Clairvaux, France, 165
Climate And Christianity, 84–87
Climate change, 75–84, 85–86
  and religion, 31–33
  and tomb building, 13–14, 39
Clonmacnoise, 19, 145–167, 152
  art, 132, 138
  high crosses, 8, 152
Clontarf, Battle of, 162
Columba, Saint, 84
Columcille of Iona, Saint, 140
Comarba, hereditary elite class, 161–2
Conn of the Hundred Battles, 109
Connachta, clan, 109
Connacht, province, 110, 148, 152
Constantine, Roman Emperor, 120, 127.
  139
Constantinople, patriarchate, 139
Cork, County, 36, 54
Cormac's Chapel, Rock of Cashel, 156,
  158
Cornwall, 28, 121
Crowley, Colm, 8
Cu Chulainn, see Setanta
Cúil Irra peninsula, County Sligo, 51
Curse of Naran-Sin, 81
Cyril of Alexandria, 139

D
Dal Riata, Scotland, 113
Danube, the river, 25
Davey, John, 9
David, King, 152, 155
de Valera, Ruaidhrí, 101
Dechitre, mother-goddess, 54

Declan, Saint, 120, 125
Dendrochronology, 77–80
Derry, County, 120
Dervorgilla, wife of O'Rourke, 167
Discovery Programme, The, 102
Dolmens, 28, 31, 39, 41–42, 48, 69
Domnach Sechnaill, church of
    Secundus, see Dunshaughlin
Dowth, tombs, 47, 57, 59, 62, 65–67,
    109
Drogheda, 59
Dublin, city, 119, 123, 167
    Hiberno-Norse Christians of, 162
Duisech, Queen of Tara, daughter of
    Tenga Umal, 114
Dumha na nGiall, see Mound of the
    Hostages
Dunchad, prince of Oriel, 167
Dunshaughlin, 120
Durrow, high crosses, 8, 152
Dyfflin, see Dublin
Dysert O'Dea, 12th Century cross, 150

E
Eamhain Mhacha, see Armagh
Early Beginnings, 24–39
Early Beliefs, 19–21
Early Christian Ireland, 125
Early Communities, 21–28
Egypt, 57, 58, 81, 89
    Coptic Church, 150
Eiscir Riada, chariot road, 145
English Church, 162
Eochaid, prince of Ulaidh, 167
Eogan, George, 60
Eoganachta, Munster tribe, 112
Ephesus, Council of, 139
Erc, Queen of Tara, daughter of
    Loarn, 113
Euphrates, the river, 37
Europe
    agriculture, 25
    art, 35, 150, 151
    Christianity, 120
    and climate change, 13, 85

    and Irish monks, 14
    Latin, use of, 17
    Megalithic cemeteries, 44, 46
    paganism, see Paganism
    popes, 160–1
    pre-historic tombs, 47
    rock carvings, 65, 154
European Church Developments, 139–
    40
    Teal, abbot of Skellig Michael, 131
Excavating Tara, 101–103

F
Fenwick, Joe, 102–3, 104–5
Flanders, 167
Flann, son of Maelseachnaill I
    High King of Ireland, 152
From The Earth To The Sky, 72–87
Finian, Saint, 130–1
Fir Bolg, 108, 109
France, 151
Franciscans, monastic monks, 166

G
Gabhra Valley, 90, 96
Gaelasius, Saint, 167
Galicia, 47
Garden of Eden, 150
Gaul, 35, 146, 148
Gaul, North see Belgae
Gaul, Saint, 155
Gavrinis, Brittany tomb, 61, 64, 66
Germany, 151
Gilla Espuic, Bishop of Limerick, 163
Global warming, see Climate change
Golden Age, of art, 153
Gothic architecture, 156
Greece, 25, 79
Greenland, 85
Germanus of Byzantium, theologian, 139
Gregory 1st, Pope. 161

H
Hale-Bopp, comet, 80–82
Harbison, Peter, 9, 148, 153–155

Harney, Lisa, 8
Henry 1st, King of England, 123
Henry II, King of England, 167
Henry IV, Emperor of Germany, 160
High Crosses, 8, 133, 148, 153, 154, 158
Horus, son of Isis, 130
Howth, 26

I
Ice-Age, 24–25, 28
Indira, Hindu god, 130
Iraq, 81
Ireland
    agriculture, 73, 123
    dwellings, 123–4
    first inhabitants, 25–28
    and Iberia, 25
    land ownership, 28–30, 123
    and the Normans, 121–2
    pre-historic landscape, 14, 26–28
    population of, 14, 28, 123
    rulers, 90
        see also Scotii
    and sea trade, 35, 36–37
    social upheaval, 13
Ireland's Pyramids, 53–57
Irish art, 20, 128–30, 133–6, 150
Irish Art In A Christian Context, 132–8
Irish Church, the, 159–63, 164
Irish Church Reform, 140
Irish language, 16
Iron Age, 36, 128
Isle of Man, 39
Ite Guennoc, tombs in Brittany, 47
Isis, Ancient Egyptian goddess, 130

J
Jeremiah, Biblical prophet, 87
Jerusalem, 139, 158
Jesus, see Christ
John of Damascus, theologian, 139
John VIII, Pope, 160
John XII, Pope, 160

K
Keltoi, people, 119
Kerry, County, 36, 67, 127
Kildare, County, 22
Killarney, 36
Knocknarea, see Maeve, Queen
Knowth, 47, 57, 59–60, 62, 64, 66–67,
    97, 109
Knowth to Mellifont, 11–23
Kilashee, Leinster, 120
Kilfenora, 12th Century cross, 150
Kilkenny, County, 120
King, Heather, 145–146, 148

L
Laighen, see Leinster
Lambay Island, 119
Latin and Irish writings, 16–17
Leaba na Cailleach, County Cork, 54
Leabhair Gabhala Erenn, 112
Lebor na hUidre, 15, 146
Leinster, province, 110, 121
Lia Fáil, 89
LiDAR, 21–23, 87, 99, 101–3
Limerick, city, 162
Limerick, County, 120
Listoghil, 48–50
Loire-Atlantique, 47
Lombards, people, 139
Lords, House of, Westminster, 166
Loughcrew, 43
Lough Derravaragh, 25
Loughshinny Harbour, 119
Louth, County, 26
Lugh, pagan god, 19, 54, 109
Lughnasa, see Lugh

M
Maeve, Queen, 48, 50, 51
Mac Aillel, Colman, Abbot of
    Clonmacnoise, 144
McCafferty, Patrick, 72–73
MacCarthys, see Eoganachta
Mac Ercae, Muirchertach, 115

MacLochlainn, Muirchertach, high king, 110, 167
MacMurrough, Dermot, King of Leinster, 167
Mac Torquil, jarl of Dublin, 167
Malachy, Saint, Armagh, 163–4, 165
Malchus, of Lismore, bishop, 163
Manannan Mac Lir, pagan god, 130
Manchan, Saint, 148
Mary, the Virgin, 130, 139, 140
Masha'llah Ibn Ahari, Persian Astrologer, 56
Mayo, County, 28
Meath, County, 67
Medieval Folklore: The Kings And Queens of Tara, 109–10
Medieval Ireland, 119–40
Mediterranean, the, 35, 146
Megalithic art, 59
Megalithic Tombs, 40–52
Melanesia, Pacific Ocean, 31
Mellifont And The Arrival of Gothic, 164–7
Mesolithic period, 38, 49–50, 96
Mesopotamia, 81
Miosgán Medhbha, see Queen Maeve
Mirror of Princes, manuscript, 90
Monasterbice, 138
Mound of the Hostages, 89, 92, 96–97, 101
Mount Hekla, Icelandic volcano, 84
Munster, province, 36, 73, 110

N
National Museum of Ireland, 35, 98
National University of Ireland, Galway, 102
Neolithic Period, 38, 41, 50, 62, 96
   Europe, 57
   farmers, 40, 73
   idols, 66
   world, 11
Neolithic Innovations: Pottery, 38–39
New Stone Age, see Neolithic period

New Testament, 154–5
Newgrange, 21, 31, 47, 54, 55, 57, 59, 62, 63–65, 79, 97, 109
   science, 55, 63–65
Newgrange, Knowth And Dowth, 57–61
Newman, Conor, 98, 100
Niall of the nine hostages, 112
Ninian, Saint, 125
Normans, arrival in Ireland, 14, 166
North Africa, 157
Notre Dame, cathedrals in France, 140

O
O'Carrigain, Tomas, 128
O'Carroll, Donough, 165
O'Connor, Rory, High King, 167
O'Cronin, Daibhi, 148, 159
O'Donoghues, see Eoganachta
Offaly, County, 31
O'Hagans, of Tullyhogue, 90
Old Testament, 154–5
Ollamh Fodhla, High King of Ireland, 87
O'Melachlainn, prince of Tara, 167
O'Neill, the, 90
O'Neills, clan, 109, 112, 155
Ó Ríordán, Seán P., 101
O'Rourke, prince of Breffni, 167
Ó Suilleabháin, Muiris, 97, 101
O'Sullivans, see Eoganachta
Orthodox Churches, 139, 140
O Maoilfhaghmhair, family, 140

P
Padre Pio, 158
Pagan To Christian, 119–24
Paganism, 19–20
Palladius, Bishop, 120
Patriarchates, of the Christian Church, 139
Patrick, Saint, 119, 120, 123, 125
Peacock, as religious symbol, 127–130
Persian Empire, 92
Picts, people, 139

Portugal, 57
Pottery, 39
Prendergast, Frank, 51–52, 58
Pyramids, *see* Egypt

R
Rahan, County Offaly, 156
Ramayana, Hindu writings, 130
Rath Breasil, synod, 163
Rathcruachain, Co Roscommon, 87
Reform and the End of Irish Church
    Independence, 159–62
Reform Gathers Pace, 162–3
Reformation, the, 167
Rhun ap Artgal, King of Strathclyde, 113
Robert the Cistercian, 165
Rock carvings, 20, 38, 65–67
    see also Stone Art
Rome, 139
    and church art, 151, 154
    and the church in Ireland, 165
    and the Irish language, 16–17
Roman Empire, 156
    and Christianity, 120, 127
Romanesque Architecture, 156–8
Roscommon, County, 28
Ross Island, *see* Killarney
Round Towers 10-12th centuries, 155
Rourke, Grellan, 132
RTE Cork, 9

S
Sagittarius, constellation, 80
Saint Brigid's Church, Co. Kildare, 164
Saint David's Monastery, Glyn Rhosyn
    Wales, 125
Saint Mullins Monastery, Carlow, 164
Saint Patrick's churchyard, 104
Sanskrit, ancient literature, 92
Saxons, tribe, 121
Scal Balb, king of the Saxons, 112
Scandinavia, 57
Scandinavians, arrival in Ireland, 19
Scotii, people, 121

Scotland
    arrivals from, 25
    and Irish invaders, 121
    pottery, 39
    trade, 35
    see also Dal Riata
Setanta, triple-born god, 19, 54, 119
Shamans, 37
Shannon, the river, 145, 146
Sheehan, John, 127, 130
Sheila-na-gig, 90
Sidhe, people of the underworld, 58
Sin, Queen of Tara, daughter of Sige son
    of Dian, 115
Skellig Michael, 21, 130–2, 164
Skyrne Valley, 77, 101
Slane, 59
Sliabh na Cailleach, 67–69, 74
    see also Cailleach
Sligo, 43
    dolmens, 28
    forests, 28
    Megalithic tombs, 8, 46, 53
    Mesolithic building tradition, 49–50
Some Queens of Tara, 111
Spain, 57, 139
Stalley, Roger, 161
Stephen VI, Pope, 160
Stone Age, 11, 13, 79, 92
    and religion, 11–12
    and tombs, 55–57, 73
Stone Age And Bronze Age Monuments
    4000 BC - 600 BC
Stone art, 31, 39, 150–1
    see also Celtic Art
Stone of Destiny, *see* Lia Fáil
Stonehenge, 8, 73
Stout, Geraldine, 61, 65–66
Syria, 139, 157

T
Tain Bo Cuailigne, 115
    see also Rathcruachain
Tara

archaeological excavations, 101–103
Banqueting Hall (Tech Mídchúarta),
   98, 99–101
Brooch, 153
Cormac's House (Tech Chormaic), 101
The Fort of the Kings (Ráith na
   Ríg), 98
Hill of, 8, 11, 21, 69, 77, 87, 89–95,
   98–101, 120
kings of, 109–10
Northern and Southern Sloping
Trenches (Clóenfherta), 98, 101
queens of, 111, 115
Ráith Ghráinne, 101
The Rath of the Synods (Ráth na
   Senad), 99, 104
Tara's Hidden Secret: Footprint of A
   Vast Enclosure, 104–5
Tara's Monuments, 92
The Content of the Cross-Panels, 150–5
The Dolmens Begin, 28–31
The Effects of Climate Change on
   Ancient Ireland, 75–84
The End of Gaelic Autonomy and the
   Arrival of The Anglo-Normans, 167
The End of Paganism, 115–117

The End of the Tomb Building Tradition
   In Ireland, 72–75
The High Crosses, 150
The Hill of Tara, 89–117
The Kingship and Landscape of Tara, 109
The Tombs of the Boyne Valley, 53–69
The Written Word, 16–19
Thomas, Julian, 8
Tigris, the river, 37
Tlaghta, near Athboy, 167
Tombs
   court tombs, 42, 57
   and land ownership, 30

megalithic tombs, 38, 39–52, 57, 67
passage tombs, 20–21, 30–31, 39, 42–
   43, 46, 47, 51, 61, 67, 73, 92, 96
portal tombs, 41, 42
tomb-builders, 12–13
wedge tombs, 41, 73
see also Dolmens
Trade Begins, 35–38
Troy, 79
Tuath, tribal territories, 159
Tuathal Teachtmar, Irish King, 120–1

U
Ui Briain, Muirteach, King of Munster,
   163
Ui Neill, see O'Neills
Ulaidh, clan, 109
Ulster, province, 110
Umm-al-Binni, lake, 81
Ussher, Archbishop James, 81

V
Valley of the Kings, see Egypt
Vance, Rob, 9
Vikings, the, 123, 131, 132, 140, 148,
   155, 162
Vinther, Bo. (Dr.), 84
Vortigen, British king, 121
Visigoths, 139
Virgin Mary, see Mary

W
Warner, Richard, 120
Wales, 28, 121, 125, 167
Waterford, city, 162, 167
Waterford, County, 125
Weather As Destiny, 31–33
Well of the White Cow, The, Tara, 89
Whithorn, Scotland, 125
Women and agriculture, 37–38

TELEVISION PROGRAMME CREDIT LIST

NARRATED BY
Phelim Drew

CHIEF HISTORICAL CONSULTANT
Dr. Peter Harbison

SPECIAL THANKS
Department of the Environment, Heritage & Local Government
The Office of Public Works
National Museum of Ireland
Royal Irish Academy

Lidar Information courtesy of Anthony Corns & Robert Shaw, Discovery Programme Ireland.
Geophysics courtesy of Discovery Programme & NUI Galway
Tara Archive Photos courtesy of UCD
Knowth Archive Photo's courtesy of Professor George Eogan & UCD
Newgrange Archive Photo's courtesy of UCC
Mike Holloway, Astronomy Ireland & Armagh Observatory
Pavel Spurny, Astronomical Institute of the Czech Academy of Sciences, SOHO (ESA & NASA)
David Brown & Queens University Belfast
George Sevastopulo, Trinity College Dublin
Neil Kearney, Trinity College Dublin
Bill MacKinnion
Jim Donnellan
John Sherlock
Archaeological Development Service, Kells.
Cairn de Gavrinis, Propriété du conseil général du Morbihan, France
Department of the Environment, Northern Ireland
TRIARC, Trinity Irish Art Research Centre
Moore Institute and Foundations of Irish Culture
Commissioners of Irish Lights
The Europe Hotel and Resort
University College Cork
Trinity College Dublin
Pat and Mary Moriarty
David Little
Noel McCluskey
Space images courtesy of Irish Astrophotography
3D scans of Durrow High Cross, courtesy of Offaly County Council, The Heritage Council and Arc Tron 3D
Skellig Michael Archive courtesy of Crossing The Line Films and the OPW
Association Renaissance de l'Abbaye de Clairvaux
Centre for Ice and Climate, Niels Bohr Institute, University of Copenhagen
Fr Tom Breen and Fr Celcus Tierney, Holy Cross Abbey
Fr Richard Purcell, Roscrea Cistercian Abbey

INSTAR Heritage Council
Volcano Archive courtesy of Sigurd Tesche / Footage Search

CONSULTANT
Rob Vance

GRELLAN D. ROURKE
Senior Conservation Architect, OPW

HEATHER KING
Archaeologist, Department of the Environment

PROF. DÁIBHÍ Ó CRÓINÍN
Historian, NUI Galway

DR. PETER HARBISON
Archaeologist, Royal Irish Academy

PROFESSOR ROGER STALLEY
Architectural Historian, Trinity College Dublin

Jean François Leroux, *Mayor of Clairvaux*
Alan Hayden, *Archaeologist*
Gavin Duffy, *Geophysicist & 3D Visualisation*
Kevin Barton, *Archaeological Geophysicist*
Dr. Thierry Daubos, *Computer Scientist, NUI Galway*
Cormac Bourke, *Archaeologist*
Professor Emeritus Mike Baillie, *Dendrochronologist, Queen's University Belfast*